The Portland Stairs Book

THE
Portland
Stairs Book

Laura O. Foster

Timber Press
Portland ▪ London

Frontispiece: At a hard-to-find dead-end, SW 10th Avenue hides a vestige of Portland's past: an old pump house for a long-gone reservoir. Wooden stairs lead uphill into steep neighborhoods with big views.

Published in 2010 by Timber Press, Inc.

The Haseltine Building
133 S.W. Second Avenue, Suite 450
Portland, Oregon 97204-3527
www.timberpress.com

2 The Quadrant
135 Salusbury Road
London NW6 6RJ
www.timberpress.co.uk

Printed in the United States of America

Library of Congress Cataloging-in-Publication Data

Foster, Laura O.
    The Portland stairs book / Laura O. Foster.
        p. cm.
    Includes bibliographical references and index.
    ISBN 978-1-60469-069-9
  1. Walking—Oregon—Portland—Guidebooks. 2. Staircases—
Oregon—Portland—Guidebooks. 3. Portland (Ore.)—Guidebooks.
I. Title.
    GV199.42.O72P67374 2010
    917.95'490444—dc22

                                                2010012481

To Cynthia Black, who gave me
a step up into the publishing world, and
to Rich Cassidy of the City of Portland, who
has gotten many Portlanders to take the stairs,
walk the sidewalks, and get out and
explore our beautiful town.

Contents

What's to Love About a Staircase?

IN PREHISTORY, the thrusting of human feet into a steep hillside resulted over time in a series of vertical footholds. These first land stairs allowed early people to traverse and inhabit new terrain. We're still building and climbing outdoor stairs for the same reasons.

Portland's topography, where peaks of up to 1,000 feet rise from near sea level, means that stairs are often the best option. Where roads cannot go, a public staircase frequently does. The most stair-rich neighborhoods are on the west side of the Willamette River, in the Tualatin Mountains, known more familiarly as the West Hills. East of the Willamette in Northeast and Southeast Portland, the changes in grade are more gradual, so stairs are less common. Notable exceptions are Alameda Ridge, an Ice Age deposit of gravels and cobbles, and two volcanic features, Mount Tabor and Rocky Butte. Their stairs are dramatic and extremely scenic. North Portland, a biker's nirvana, is, frankly, under-endowed in the stair department.

Many of Portland's public staircases were built in the era before cars. As the city grew in the early 1900s, land was developed further from downtown. New neighborhoods were not viable,

Looking down from NW Summit Avenue to the quiet dead-end of Lovejoy Street.

from a real estate sales standpoint, unless they were connected to town by a streetcar; as a result streetcar lines crisscrossed the city. When a new development such as The Alameda or Westover Terraces was planned, residents needed a quick way to descend from their hillside homes to the nearest streetcar line, and stairs were the solution. Even today, at the bottom or top of many hillside staircases is a bus stop, a vestige of the streetcars and the stops associated with them.

Midcentury, staircases were built to help heal rifts in urban neighborhoods as thoroughfares such as Front Avenue (now Naito Parkway) and McLoughlin Boulevard were built, cutting off vehicular access to intersecting streets. There are many steps from this era in South Portland. The stairs allowed pedestrians, at least, to continue on long-used transit routes.

I first fell in love with stairs when I left flat Chicagoland and attended college in Dubuque, Iowa. Dubuque is a Mississippi River hill town, in an area bypassed by the glaciers that dragged the topographical interest out of much of the Midwest. Sunday afternoons, before diving back into the books, I'd wander around town looking for likely dead-ends that might harbor a staircase down the river bluff. Stairs, I'd discovered, were a good refuge from the wailings of REO Speedwagon that pervaded the dorm.

When I moved to Portland in the 1980s I began exploring my new town. One day I encountered a staircase ascending from NE Wistaria Drive at the base of Alameda Ridge. I hesitated. There was no one around to ask. Is it private? Where does it go? When caught trespassing I've had good luck with the ignorance defense, so I took that first step up to investigate. One hundred seventeen steps later, I felt pretty sure that I was not on private property, and found that things looked different up there. Bigger houses, broader view. That same sense of discovery, intrigue, and delight still greets me at the foot of every staircase.

There is something ineffably "other" about a neighborhood staircase. It's not a road. Not a trail. Not a multi-use path. A staircase is a tangible concession that no, indeed, roads cannot be carved wherever humans want them. Their slightly subversive, escapist nature attracts urban explorers, runners, walkers, and anyone else who cannot comprehend how mall-walking could be a pleasurable activity.

Portland has a significant number of public staircases, 196 according to the list kept by the city's Office of Transportation. (That list doesn't include park stairs, school stairs, or private-but-accessible-to-the-public stairs.) San Francisco, in comparison, has more than 600, many of which are in the wonderful book *San Francisco Stairway Walks*.

You will find lots of ways to explore Portland's stairs in my book. Because everyone loves a list, "Staircases in the Extreme" highlights stairways that are superlative in one way or another, though despite a friend's suggestion, I didn't include the best stairs for kissing because I really couldn't speak to that. The segments in "Stairs with a Story" feature staircases or areas with stairs that lead you into the city's history. They include streetcar steps, landscape stairs in parks, steps hanging off river bridges, and citizen-built steps along unused rights-of-way in hilly Southwest Portland. Here you'll also find a list of staircases with 100 steps or more. "Public Spaces, Grand Staircases" takes you inside and up the stairs of four historic buildings—great public places every Portlander should know.

The five stairway treks, each with an accompanying map, lead you on urban excursions that contain hundreds of steps in different areas of town. Some walks stay in one neighborhood, such as Mount Tabor. The Alameda Ridge walk, on the other hand, travels much of the ridge's length, which includes several neighborhoods: Sabin, Alameda, Beaumont, and Rose City Park.

The stair list at the back of the book covers Portland's street stairs, Willamette River bridge stairs, and significant park stairs. A total of 207 public exterior staircases, or 10,155 steps, are on the list. These numbers don't include the many private steps (Meridian Ridge, Lewis and Clark College, or adidas) or interior public steps that are featured elsewhere in the book.

While this book is comprehensive, it's not exhaustive: some Portland stairs are left for you to discover. Let me know what you find; you can email me at Laura@portlandhillwalks.com.

To get to a staircase via public transit, www.trimet.org will show you the way. Also useful are walking maps, one for each section of Portland, that are published by the city's Office of Transportation. Order them at www.gettingaroundportland.org or call the city at 503-823-5490.

Lastly: did I walk every stair in this book? I did!

Staircases in the Extreme:
Longest, Oldest, and Other Superlative Stairs

Longest

Portland's longest staircase, using a strict interpretation (meaning no roads, paths, or long stretches of sidewalks between flights) is the Elevator Stairs, 203 wooden steps in 13 flights between SW Broadway Drive and Hoffman Avenue. The longest set of stairs, 18 flights broken by paths, sidewalks, and roads, is 282 steps, at Mount Tabor. The world's longest stairway, listed by the Guinness Book of Records, is at the century-old Niesenbahn funicular railway near Spiez, Switzerland. While only employees can climb its 11,674 steps (total elevation gain: 5,476 feet), it is open one day each June to 200 people for the annual Niesenlauf stair run.

Oldest

Of the 196 staircases on the City of Portland's list of public stairways, 120 have known construction dates. From this list, the oldest staircase dates from 1910. It's 41 steps up from SW Montgomery Drive at 1698 to Vista Avenue. Many older staircases, once made of wood, have been replaced with concrete or aluminum; their original dates are unknown. In Washington Park,

Eighty-six steps lead from SW Montgomery Drive up to Greenway Avenue.

the 280 steps rambling uphill from SW 24th and Burnside surely predate 1900. An elderly Douglas fir that has reclaimed one of the landings is just one example of how nature is inexorably absorbing these steps; in 500 years they'll be merely a limey layer in the soil profile.

Newest
Built in 2008, 51 steps rise from NW Glisan at 24th to Westover alongside condominiums. On this hill from 1895 to 1971 patients at Saint Vincent Hospital looked out over the city.

Steepest
For ergonomic and safety reasons, most stairs comply with certain measurements, for example a tread width of 9 inches and a riser height between 5 and 8 inches. Not too steep, not too narrow, and people can climb a staircase on autopilot. Some stairs in Portland, however, make you pay attention.

From Reservoir 6 up to Reservoir 5 in Mount Tabor Park, one 96-step flight in this 134-step heart-thumper is unrelieved by a landing. To add tension to an already edgy staircase, the steps are so steep and narrow you will gain new respect for the humble handrail.

On Alameda Ridge one morning, after climbing and descending most of its 805 steps, I had gotten in a stair walking groove, until the 8-inch high risers in a staircase at NE 50th and Wistaria made me feel I was about to pitch forward on the descent. Most other stairs on the ridge are hand-height tall (that's my hand, and that's about 6.5 inches). After climbing more than 10,000 steps in the city, I discovered at least one thing: not all stairs are created equal. Sometimes a situation requires a bit of deviance from the ideal. Isn't life like that?

Grandest, Inexplicably

From SE Ankeny down into a backwater of Southeast Portland's Laurelhurst Park is a grand brick staircase of 88 steps. My guess for its existence stems from the fact that the nearby mansion at 3360 SE Ankeny was built in 1912 for a Portland mayor, H. Russell Albee; these stairs complement the home's architecture and perhaps are an example of mayoral pork.

Best People-Watching

My favorite spot in town for reading, eating, or reclining outside is on the broad grass steps of the Washington Park Amphitheater. Bring sunglasses for discreet observations of passersby; the stage there seems to inspire random acts of personal expression, from ballet to declamations to tap-dancing. During annual free concerts, picnicking on these steps is one of Portland's many sweet summer delights.

Most Refined

The elevated walk at the southeast corner of SW Vista and Spring leads to a staircase of 71 steps. Formal retaining walls, an elegant balustrade, impeccable landscaping, and of course, steps, all contribute to the ambience in one of the city's prettiest neighborhoods, Portland Heights. Lots of nearby stairs could make for a morning of stair climbing.

Soberest

A long, stately staircase in Mount Calvary Cemetery with 113 steps. Climb to the altar at the top of the hill on a foggy day and watch the metaphors arise from the mist. The staircase is north of West Burnside, just to the east of where Skyline Boulevard splits off.

Washington Park Amphitheater's grassy steps, ideal for picnics and cloud-gazing, and small walking steps that traverse them.

Most Privately Public
Steps from NW Luray Terrace to Luray Circus serve a dead-end with just three homes on it. On these little-traveled stairs, a colony of mushrooms grew undisturbed one wet October. It's a circus because it's a circle.

Most Publicly Private
At SW 48th and Burnside is a long, steep staircase of wood and aluminum, beautifully designed and tempting. Admire from a distance. Near it is a 1940 tunnel with the same rustic stonework seen on Rocky Butte. Both the tunnel and Rocky Butte were work relief projects.

Fishiest
A salmon jostling its fellow fish upstream could relate to the scene on the interior steps at Powell's Burnside during the holidays, with the run peaking on weekend afternoons. Whether you're climbing or descending, you're swimming against the current.

Most Likely to be Inhabited
Steps and subterranean walkways under SW Kelly and the Ross Island Bridge approaches, and at SW Grover, become urban campgrounds in wet weather.

Safest
The outdoor steel towers at the Ecotrust building at NW 10th and Irving were added in 2001 to provide structural and seismic stabilization to an 1895 brick warehouse. Stairs integrated into them lead to a rare opportunity for balcony-level views in the Pearl. Get some pizza, climb up, and enjoy the scene. Doors to the staircase are open during weekday business hours.

The authoritative arrow on these steps leading to an underground passage was not enough to convince me to disturb the men sleeping there early one Sunday morning.

Most Accessible

At the Peninsula Park Sunken Rose Garden, two of the six 1913 staircases leading down into the garden were re-engineered as ramps in 2008, with their brickwork laid in a pattern identical to the original steps. From a distance, the ramps are indistinguishable from the staircases.

Most Perplexing

Two staircases hanging off the Morrison Bridge westbound laboriously route pedestrians down, then under a hanging roadbed, then up again. The humans have to negotiate 50-plus noisy and unpleasant steps so that an automobile would not have to stop at a pedestrian crossing.

PORTLAND STAIR FACTS

Portland's Office of Transportation maintains the city's public, non-park, non-bridge stairs. Most are concrete. Older ones are wood; when their time comes, they may not be replaced with wood, according to Steve Yates, an engineer with the city.

More than a few staircases in town are aluminum. These often appear to float, such as steps appended to a bridge deck. Some aluminum staircases have nonskid material on their

A South Portland street, once a through-way, is now a dead-end due to the transformation of Front Avenue (now Naito) into a thoroughfare in the 1940s. Stairs like these help pedestrians negotiate a tricky landscape with many dead-ends that stymie automobiles.

treads; the Thurman Street Bridge staircase has punched aluminum treads. The rough tread, combined with the abrading action of footsteps, help chew up leaves so they can blow away or fall through the holes. Soggy leaves are a hazard on city stairs in the fall.

Stairs are not only a transit easement. Often, buried beneath or attached to them are utilities such as water and sewer lines. Any new staircases in town are built by developers who are required to provide pedestrian access through or adjacent to their development, such as the Meridian Ridge steps which provide pedestrian access through the Audubon Center's trails up the hill to Skyline Boulevard and beyond. Another new staircase is at the dead-end of NW Glisan, built by the developer of the nearby condominiums on NW Westover Place.

Unlike city sidewalks, which the city owns, but homeowners must pay to maintain, the city will make and pay for stairway improvements to public stairs adjacent to (or in one case, running through) a homeowner's property. Periodic maintenance is by city crews, but judging from the plant debris often seen on the steps, is probably not frequent enough. Homeowners often step up to care for neighborhood staircases.

■.■.■.■.

Stairs with a Story:
Twenty Mini-Explorations Up, Down, and Around Town

BESIDES LEADING TO good views, a staircase can be a portal into Portland's past. Some of the stories in this section are big: a neighborhood destroyed and rebuilt, or a Depression-era project that relieved joblessness while creating a beautiful monument.

Some of the stories, of mushrooms or century-old garbage cans, are small. For me, these minute observations are a joy. Like a gold watch found under a pile of leaves—they're unexpected, they're worth treasuring, and they're free to those who keep their eyes open.

Portland's Century Stairs:
Twenty Staircases with 100 Steps or More

New Hampshire's White Mountains have 48 peaks over 4,000 feet. To join the Four Thousand Footer Club, you must climb them all. Portland is a bit more laid back. All it takes to be in our One Hundred Stepper Club is to climb 20 staircases that each have at least 100 steps, for a total of 3,144 steps! Big views at the top are the reward.

The 146 steps up from busy SW Barbur Boulevard transition from a gritty urban staircase to a vertical oasis on their way to a secluded neighborhood in the hills.

1. *282 steps:* Mount Tabor Park, SE 69th dead-end south of Yamhill to Mount Tabor summit. Good for a workout with lots of landings.

2. *280 steps:* Washington Park, Stearns Road steps at SW 24th Place and Burnside to the *Coming of the White Man* statue. From the park's earliest days; funky, varied, and fun.

3. *203 steps:* SW Broadway Drive to Hoffman (Elevator Stairs). Reputedly replaced an elevator that ascended the cliff here.

4. *179 steps:* SW Cardinell at 12th to upper Cardinell. A nasty false summit.

5. *176 steps:* NW 107th Avenue in Linnton. One of many ways to climb around in Linnton.

6. *175 steps:* Washington Park, SW Osage to Lewis and Clark Drive. Good workout steps: clean and even with no distractions.

7. *167 steps:* NW Meridian Ridge Drive to Skyline Boulevard. One of the biggest views in town.

8. *157 steps:* NW Summit Avenue to Westover. Steep and busy, with benches for resting.

9. *152 steps:* SW Market Street Drive to Mill Street Terrace. Ends atop the Highway 26 tunnels through the West Hills.

10. *146 steps:* SW Barbur Boulevard at Parkhill to Parkhill Drive (Nebraska Steps). A split personality: refined on top, businesslike below.

11. *145 steps:* SW Terwilliger Boulevard at Condor Lane to VA Hospital. Gracious, with landings before you even need them.

12. *136 steps:* Jackson Middle School to SW 41st at Galeburn Street. Middle schoolers using these can eat all the Cheetos they want.

13. *134 steps:* Mount Tabor Park in Southeast Portland, Reservoir 6 to 5. Steep; hang on.

14. *131 steps:* NW Fairfax west of Cumberland and Westover intersection to Cumberland. An adjacent homeowner once had a mechanical bird that tweeted as you passed by, cheering the weary climber.

15. *129 steps:* SW Iowa Street dead-end west of View Point Terrace into greenspace and George Himes Park. Step out of the neighborhood and into the forest.

16. *127 steps:* NE Wistaria at 4131 to Alameda. Morning runners and talkers abound.

17. *118 steps:* NE Wistaria at 4243 to Alameda. A circuit with the stairway adjacent.

18. *106 steps:* Highway 30, north of NW 105th Avenue to 2nd Street in Linnton. Leads to Linnton School Place, a public school turned condominiums.

19. *101 steps:* NW Thurman to Aspen. Bamboo gone wild.

20. *100 steps:* SW Custer Way from LaView to Kelly. Ross Island views at the top.

Willamette River Bridge Stairs

Well, it seemed an easy task to find the bridge stairs: there'd be one staircase on each side of the river. Right? Not the case. The Broadway Bridge has two staircases leading up from Naito Parkway, and two more from approach streets, so that's four on just the west side. It's the same situation for the Morrison and the Hawthorne bridges. Some bridges, however, like the Sellwood Bridge, have only one staircase on each side of the river. The Ross Island Bridge has none, unless I missed them. And the Fremont and Marquam bridges, as interstate highway bridges, allow no pedestrian traffic, so no stairs.

While walking on the Eastbank Esplanade looking for bridge stairs, I glanced up under the Morrison Bridge to see a staircase that looked like M. C. Escher designed it; it descended from the bridge deck, made a turn, and then ascended, never making it all the way to the ground! There are a few of these hanging stairs on the east side, designed to help pedestrians negotiate ramps where cars are accelerating and there are no crosswalks.

My favorites are the two identical Broadway Bridge staircases rising from NW Naito Parkway southbound, hands-down the

The Broadway Bridge and steps up to it from NW Naito Parkway.

best looking bridge staircases in town, with a bit of New Orleans attitude.

Another good one is the Steel Bridge staircase that rises from NW Naito Parkway, northbound. If you're used to walking the Esplanade–Waterfront Park loop, you know that the loop feeds walkers onto the lower deck of the Steel Bridge. This staircase lifts you to the bridge's upper deck where the creosote smell is absent, and the views are great.

All in all, there are 1,098 steps on Portland's Willamette River bridges. The beautiful Saint Johns Bridge in North Portland has no stairs on the bridge proper but an elegant 41-step staircase floats down the hill below it. The steps are in Cathedral Park.

Steps to Show Out of Town Visitors: The Westover Terraces Steps

These steps, in the Hillside neighborhood in Northwest Portland, date from a 1910s development called Westover Terraces. It's a wondrous neighborhood carved from the face of the West Hills by a water cannon that sluiced away unwanted rocks, soil, and vegetation in order to create level streets and home sites. The neighborhood's face to the city is elegant, with grand homes and some of Portland's prettiest staircases. Wander back far enough, however, and it gets even better: several manicured streets such as Cumberland and Macleay end abruptly at trails into 5,000-acre Forest Park. From there, you can access the 30-mile-long Wildwood Trail into the backcountry of northwest Multnomah County.

❖ ❖ ❖

The Lovejoy to Summit steps are the lowest and shortest staircase in Westover Terraces, but the most elegant, framed by trees, with a backdrop of a rustic stone wall.

The staircases are:

- Lovejoy dead-end west of Marcia Avenue to Summit: 33 steps. Across from the top, a private staircase made of stone is noteworthy. One of the prettiest dead-ends in town.

- Summit Avenue south of Summit Court to Westover Terrace: 157 steps, with a rain gutter.

- Cornell Road at 2832 to Summit Avenue: 73 steps, with a rain gutter in the rail.

- Fairfax Terrace to Cumberland Road: 131 steps.

- Luray Terrace to Luray Circus: 52 steps.

Rocky Butte's Grand Staircase

Rocky Butte is a volcanic cinder cone in Northeast Portland, east of 82nd Avenue. The butte's grand staircase of local basalt was constructed in the mid to late 1930s by men employed by the WPA (Works Progress Administration), a federal government program that hired 25,000 people in Portland alone to help relieve the financial anguish and hopelessness of the Great Depression.

The Rocky Butte Scenic Drive, like most WPA projects, was labor intensive, designed to keep the maximum number of men employed for the maximum length of time. Despite the largely unskilled workforce, the result is a work of art. Since 1991, the drive has been on the National Register of Scenic Places.

Beginning on the west side of the butte, the drive winds up

This sweeping staircase leads to Rocky Butte's fortress peak, a lawn-covered lookout over Portland. Views to the east on a clear day include Cascade mountains and the Columbia River Gorge.

the 600-foot peak. The rock for the railings, bollards, and walls (some of which are up to 42 feet high and 1,500 feet long) was hand-hewn in a style sometimes called Oregon Rustic. It came from a quarry on the east side of the butte, an area now popular with rock climbers.

The style of the rockwork is the same style seen at Timberline Lodge, and at the spectacular entrance portals of the Burnside and Cornell Road tunnels, all of which were Depression-era work relief projects. The Scenic Drive also includes a 375-foot-long tunnel that switchbacks through the butte. It was hand-excavated.

At the top, the 72-step grand staircase leads to a viewpoint fortress with a 360-degree view. Rocky Butte is the western portal to the Columbia River Gorge drive that was popularized with the creation of the Columbia River Highway in 1917.

The staircase and viewpoint are in Joseph Wood Hill Park, two acres inside the larger Rocky Butte Natural Area managed by Portland Parks. Joseph Wood Hill operated Hill Military Academy on the butte for years, at the site now occupied by City Bible Church.

Another WPA project visible from the top of Rocky Butte is the Portland International Airport. Workers began filling a Columbia River slough there in the 1930s to prepare the land for an airport, when it became clear that the Swan Island Airport, on an island in the Willamette River, was rapidly becoming inadequate.

Steps to Sit On

I like marginal places, so stairs are pleasant places to be: not here, not there, but connected to both. Instead of being just a quickly passing transient on a public staircase, it's fun to sit down and watch what and who passes. Many stairs are busy with runners, chatty friends, lunchtime exercisers, and I've heard, deer and coyote, who know a good route when they see one.

While waiting out an October shower under a cedar on some Alameda Ridge stairs, I watched a rat and a jay share some French fries about ten steps above me. A runner with a dog scared them into the ivy. Five or ten minutes passed and the rain kept me tucked under the cedar. The street below gleamed and it was pleasant watching the occasional bus and cars from my hidden vantage.

Soon, a large orange cat ran down the stairs with a rat in its mouth.

The rain eased up, and I climbed on, happy to have been there.

A good-sitting staircase has a view, plenty of foot traffic, a tucked-away feeling, and no bad smells. Here are three of the best:

- NE Fremont at 3011 to Alameda Terrace. This staircase's many landings and flights stagger up Alameda Ridge in a pleasing way. It's close to Alameda School, so afternoons are busy.

- NW Fairfax at Westover to Cumberland. These long steps have a welcome sidewalk midway with a bench provided by a hospitable homeowner. The landscaping is beautiful.

- Rose Garden steps in Washington Park. Recessed into the walls of these formal steps are stone benches that make a great spot to listen to the parade of summertime tourists talk about Portland.

A home on an Alameda Ridge staircase.

Roses and the Steps that Frame Them

In Portland, roses are iconic. Peninsula Park in North Portland's Piedmont neighborhood includes the city's first public rose garden, constructed in 1909. The formally designed two-acre garden is sunken below the surrounding street grade, and accessed by stairs at each of the four compass points. The stairs, topped by a classical balustrade of cast concrete, lead you down into a magical, secret place, unseen by passing vehicles on nearby streets.

The Washington Park International Rose Test Garden is the largest of Portland's three public rose gardens (Ladd's Addition

The Peninsula Park Rose Garden is sunken and accessed by elegant staircases. The staircase in the foreground has been converted to an accessible brick ramp, in a pattern matching its partner opposite. A sign at the top warns visitors of the steep 11 percent grade.

is the third). Located just west of downtown in SW Portland's King's Hill neighborhood, it is the city's most famous garden, and a visitor favorite.

In Washington Park, staircases lead visitors down, down, and down into the four-acre garden, from the top level where a steady stream of tour buses park, to the Queens Walk at the garden's lowest level. The garden was created in 1917 on land once terraced to provide home sites. The many staircases and stone paths create a linear hardscape that contrasts beautifully with the effusive blooms that appear from late spring until mid-fall.

Both gardens are places to bring visitors and a picnic. You can't go wrong with good food, friends, roses, and stairs.

Reservoir Steps of Washington Park

Like the three open-air reservoirs on Mount Tabor, Washington Park's two open-air reservoirs have held treated drinking water since 1895. Water constantly flushes through them on its way to Portland taps. For the occasional bird droppings into the water, "dilution is the solution" as one Water Bureau employee succinctly noted.

The open reservoirs' working life is to come to an end by 2014, to comply with EPA regulations. Portland had requested a variance from the regulations, but in January 2010 it was denied. The plan is that those on Mount Tabor will remain open, but no longer on line. Washington Park's Reservoir 3 will be capped and continue functioning as a working reservoir. Reservoir 4, below it, will not.

The reservoirs remain a major historic attraction of the park. When built, walkways around them encouraged strollers. By the 1940s, fears of sabotage ended that practice and a chain link

Reservoir 3 at Washington Park, one of the last working open-air reservoirs in the nation. The iron bars in the foreground have separated the water from pedestrians since 1895. The white liner in the reservoir (seen on the left, above the water line) aids in water retention and ease of cleaning. The gatehouse, like those on Mount Tabor, is concrete made to resemble stone.

fence was installed, significantly marring the beauty of the site. In 2009, new iron fencing, in the style of the original fencing alongside the reservoirs, replaced the chain link. The 50-step staircase down into the reservoir bowl was reopened, and pedestrians were again welcome.

Along the east side of the reservoir is a staircase with permeable pavement at the landings and adjacent sidewalks. It has 49 steps.

A Stair Hunt in Washington Park

Portland has beautiful public parks on both sides of the river, but nothing beats Washington Park for size, variety of terrain and topics, and beauty. This park's oldest acreage was purchased by the City of Portland from Amos King in 1870. More than 25 stairways climb the hills in its older section alone. Several of Washington Park's staircases are featured throughout this chapter (in "Portland's Century Stairs," "Roses and the Steps that Frame Them," and "Reservoir Steps of Washington Park") and included in the parks section of the stairways list at the back of the book. A map of the park can be downloaded from www.washingtonparkpdx.org.

Small discoveries along the way are the best part of a stair hunt. Here are a few places to start:

- Along SW Wright Avenue and the hillside to the east. This is where the zoo animals were once housed. Stairs appear suddenly, their purpose now a mystery.

◾◾ The Japanese Garden. The stairs leading up into the garden invite you to contemplate your steps and slow your pace. The garden also occupies an earlier site of the zoo. Like the zoo, the Japanese Garden charges an admission fee, but the steps are free.

◾◾ The Park Place entrance steps. Just west of SW Vista Avenue, these formal, brick steps lead to a great old fashioned playground with big-swinging swings and tall slides. Beverly Cleary used to wax the slides in Grant Park with wax paper to make them go faster. These slides would be an excellent place to try that technique. Picnic tables, a nice lawn, and the Sacagawea statue in this area make a great kid-outing.

A scenic entrance to Washington Park at the end of SW Marconi Avenue. Behind the foliage a stairway hides.

Willamette Heights Stairs and the 1905 World's Fair Below

Willamette Heights, a hilly neighborhood beyond Balch Creek Canyon in Northwest Portland, is tied to the 1905 world's fair in the flats below. The fair, also known as the Lewis and Clark Exposition, took place around Guilds Lake, a natural lake in what is now the Guilds Lake Industrial Sanctuary (the lake has been filled), and was designed to attract investment and population to Portland. One of the fair's backers, Robert Livingstone, was also employed by a company that sought to develop Willamette Heights, which had been platted in 1887 but not successfully built out. To stimulate home sales, it was arranged that trolleys which brought people to the fair would travel a leg over the Thurman Street Bridge to check out the big views of Cascade peaks, and not incidentally, lots for sale in the heights. The sales pitch must have been effective because many fairgoers moved permanently to Portland and enough of them moved into Willamette Heights to populate the neighborhood.

Livingstone hired architect Emil Schacht and the result is one of Portland's earliest and densest concentrations of spectacular Arts and Crafts homes. Several streets dead-end onto Forest Park trails, and the remote aspect of this neighborhood makes it unique in Portland.

❖ ❖ ❖

Stairs to investigate are:

- NW Thurman Street at 3418 to NW Aspen Street: 101 steps. The urban wilderness factor increases as you climb.

The Thurman Street Bridge was built in 1904. Beyond its west end is geographically isolated Willamette Heights, cut off from the rest of town by this canyon, a ridge, and Forest Park. Steps lead down from the bridge into the canyon. On the left, unseen, beautiful Balch Creek runs out of the mountains free until it is culverted underground at the point seen in the image.

- NW Thurman at 33rd: this 25-step wooden staircase heads downhill to a path and a public right-of-way down to Vaughn. I couldn't find the lower half, and didn't snoop, though it is listed on www.portlandmaps.com as a right-of-way.

- NW Vaughn dead-end at 30th: 32 concrete steps lead to a path on the hillside. The path takes you to an upper dead-end of Vaughn. From there, exploring the scenic streets at Willamette Heights' far reaches is a treat. Come back down and find good food options along NW Vaughn and Thurman—it makes for a great evening out.

A Stair with a (Small) View

A big view from the top of a stairway is one of the best things in life that are free, especially when the clouds are putting on a show, as they often do in Portland in October and March. Other stair views are as rewarding but more subtle: glimpses into manicured back yards, a stair tunnel made of bamboo or laurel, the architecture of a staircase as it fits itself into the landscape. A slow pace, with stops, squats, and turnarounds, will reward you with the micro tableaux found on risers, mossy walls, and leaf-covered treads.

Most of the "Century Stairs" on pages 25 to 28 offer big views. Here are some that offer the small view, sometimes on the stairs, sometimes in the area just beyond.

Creston Park's grove of beech trees glows on an autumn day.

- SW 42nd Avenue at Garden Home Road to Garden Home north of Hume. These stairs, in an area that was half rural/half urban when settled, are a delight, with hand-hewn basalt walls alongside 48 steps that lead to a charming street.

- SW Vista Avenue north of 1636. These 67 steps travel downhill next to a vacant lot, with wonderful views into Goose Hollow and beyond.

- SW Tichner at Parkside Lane. These 23 steps climb into a narrow lane lined with beautiful homes. Adjacent to the steps is a private staircase that earned a spot on the National Register of Historic Places for the artistry of the basalt walls and steps.

- Creston Park in Southeast Portland. This lovely park sits in a bowl, with stairs leading down from Powell, and a grand staircase up from the swimming pool that takes you to a magnificent, and rare in Portland, grove of old beech trees.

Marquam Hill Steps for Wellness

Mental health comes from exercising your brain with complicated tasks, and finding the staircases on this steep hillside above SW Terwilliger Boulevard qualifies. Marquam Hill's corrugated landscape is overlain with an aerial walkway, a tram, and stairs galore. The hill is home to Oregon Health and Science University and The Portland Veterans Administration Medical Center.

Only one Marquam Hill staircase is on the Portland stairways list: SW Condor Lane at Terwilliger Boulevard to the VA Medical Center grounds. One of the most beautiful staircases in

Steps from SW Condor Lane at Terwilliger Boulevard ascend through the forest to the grounds of the Veterans Administration Medical Center.

town, it travels uphill through a forest in a stately manner, though it ends, disappointingly, at a parking lot.

Below are a few other staircases on the hill. From them, explore onward. Don't miss the ninth-floor patio at the top of the aerial tram, and the long, covered walkway between OHSU Hospital and the VA Medical Center.

The OHSU Web site (www.ohsu.edu) has a campus map and list of cafés. Before leaving home, you may want to download both. Walking around Marquam Hill is not a relaxing experience: the topography is confusing, the buildings enormous and often in the path of where you want to head. But it's a fascinating one.

- SW 9th and Gaines down to Veterans Park Road: 123 steps running downhill alongside the School of Nursing.

- SW Sam Jackson Parkway down alongside BICC (Biomedical Information Communication Center): 63 steps.

Citizen-Made Stairs

In hilly Southwest Portland, especially beyond Council Crest, streets don't adhere to a linear grid, and many streets were platted but never built out due to the steep terrain. In the 1990s, a group of Southwest neighbors formed SW Trails to turn these unused public rights-of-way into paths. One of their goals was to stop the vacating process, whereby adjacent property owners were able to privatize a once-public right-of-way, and to help kids avoid walking on busy roads on their way to school or play. In Southwest, 85 percent of local streets don't have side-

At SW 45th Avenue and Beaverton-Hillsdale Highway, SWTrails has created a rough staircase leading out of the neighborhoods above, down to the highway. The stairs, combined with a stop-lighted pedestrian crossing, enable kids heading to nearby schools to keep out of their parents' cars and on their own feet.

walks. Streets without curbs are not uncommon; streets without paving are not either.

The Peaks and Valleys Staircase Excursion on page 87 traverses some of the steps built and paths hewn from the vegetation by SW Trails. Another great little exploration combining stairs, water, and trails, courtesy of SW Trails, is to start at SW Lee's dead-end west of 42nd Avenue. A trail and steps lead over a creek to 43rd; from there, take a trail from Admiral Court's dead-end over a creek to 45th Avenue, north of Beaverton-Hillsdale Highway. This water is a tributary of Fanno Creek, one of the area's most urban streams. It starts from small streams like these in Portland's West Hills and runs 15 miles through Portland, Beaverton, Tigard, and Durham before joining the Tualatin River in Tualatin.

Linnton's Elevated Sidewalks and Commuter Stairs

Linnton used to be a stand-alone town of sawmills, a smelter, a meat cannery, and other industries. By 1915, it was incorporated into Portland. The town's fortunes eventually waned, and by the 1940s, Linnton's most prosperous days were behind it. Still, even then, a downtown thrived along Highway 30, with a butcher shop, pharmacy, department store, grocery, and barber shop among other retail establishments. Up the hill, residents lived, walked to work, and sent their children to a neighborhood public school.

The town was irreparably altered in the 1960s when Highway 30, a federal highway, was widened through town. Highway 30's west side businesses were flush up against the base of the hills. To widen the road, they had to be removed, and the base of the hillside dynamited.

An elevated sidewalk in Linnton resulted from road-widening in the 1960s.
On the right are several private staircases to homes on the hill above.

The result was the loss of Linnton's central core. The school closed in 1970. Today, Linnton's staircases, once trod by workers heading downhill to jobs along the river, are some of the most interesting in town, as they lead uphill, crossing steep, often one-lane streets. Several staircases end along elevated sidewalks created from the road widening. Along these elevated walks are many beautiful private staircases as well, the moss growing or absent on them betraying how much use they receive.

A few of Linnton's staircases:

- Saint Helens Road (Highway 30) north of 105th Avenue to 2nd Street dead-end: 106 steps.

- 2nd Street at 108th Avenue to 3rd Street: 92 steps.

Playing on Stairs at the Keller and Lovejoy Fountains

The Ira Keller Fountain was built in 1969 and christened the Forecourt Fountain for its setting in front of the Civic Auditorium; the original idea was to create a park that would be a combination courtyard and automobile turnaround for Auditorium patrons. The fountain's name was changed in 1978 to honor Keller who, as the first head of the Portland Development Commission, created the city's first urban renewal district here, the South Auditorium District.

The former neighborhood here, South Portland, had been the landing spot for thousands of Italian and Eastern European

Jewish immigrants from the late 1890s to about 1920. In the suburban-focused 1950s, it and other inner city neighborhoods were scruffy and seen as having outlived their design life. By 1963, 54 blocks of homes, businesses, and synagogues were razed and construction commenced on a series of towers for residential and commercial use. Fountains and parks were to have been the sparkling tiaras on the modern urban neighborhood.

But when the city hired landscape architect Lawrence Halprin, ideas began to evolve. Halprin envisioned parks not for looking at or as backdrops for the buildings around them, but as places for people to play, even dance (his wife, Anna, a choreographer, influenced his designs, and both fountains have stagelike

Ira Keller Fountain sans water, looking west.

platforms at their bases). The Forecourt Fountain was designed in Halprin's firm by Angela Danadjieva. Its flowing water and precipices are evocative of mountain cascades. The Lovejoy Fountain was installed first, in 1966, along with Pettygrove Park one block away. Lovejoy Fountain's severe hardscape is evocative of the spare landforms created by erosion in Oregon's high desert. More tucked away in the urban renewal area, it is less known by today's Portlanders than the more prominently placed Ira Keller Fountain.

When the Forecourt Fountain was dedicated in 1969, Halprin joined the crowd in rolling up his trousers and wading in it, to the dismay of a much more conservative Portland establishment at that time. The fountain was derided then as a place where hippies would wash their feet. This was at the height of the Generation Gap era when distrust and enmity existed between people under 30 and "the establishment." Despite the sniffing of some newspaper editorialists, the public loved the fountains.

The fountains are no longer the focus of as much civic attention, but they are historic, for their connection with the pioneering designs of Halprin, who died in 2009, and for their role in the city's history of urban renewal. With their steep faces and unfenced clifflike elements, they are a throwback to times when fear of litigation did not rule design or recreation.

Bike-Friendly Stairs

Bikes and stairs aren't a great match, especially if you ride one of those cushy but lumbering city cruisers, but a few staircases in town help smooth the bumps.

The staircase hanging from the east end of the Burnside Bridge has a gutter on the side of the treads. Set the bike wheel

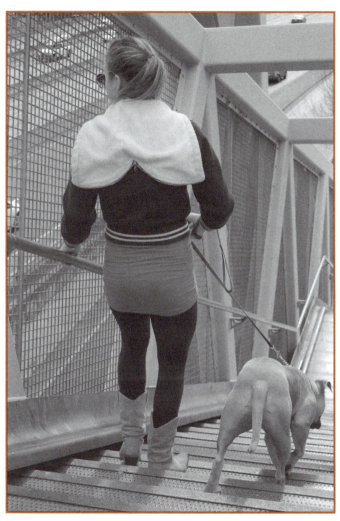

The stairs leading from the Burnside Bridge to the Vera Katz Eastbank Esplanade, and their bike gutter to aid bike commuters.

in it, and walk your bike down, bump-free. This is a premier gutter, curving and commodious, that was built when the staircase went in.

Kudos also to Portland's Office of Transportation for a clever adaptation to an existing staircase. At the SW Galeburn Street steps between 40th and 41st Avenues, angle iron was attached to the concrete balustrade, on the edge of the treads, so kids at Jackson Middle School can wheel their bikes over the steps.

Of the 200 or so staircases I researched for this book, I noticed gutters on only one other: SW 5th at Barbur Boulevard in the South Burlingame neighborhood.

A staircase to be built on Waud Bluff connecting North Portland residents to Swan Island jobs will have a bike gutter on it. That staircase and accompanying path will provide a much-needed non-car access to Swan Island.

Wooden Stairs and Sidewalks

Most public stairs are concrete, but that wasn't always the case. Sawmills used to mill wood for wooden sidewalks and stairways. Beginning in the early 1900s, Portland began to replace its wooden sidewalks with concrete. But there are two wooden sidewalks left to investigate, at Greenway Avenue and on the Thurman Street Bridge, and both have stairs connected to them.

Take the 86-step wooden staircase at SW Montgomery Drive at 2860 up to Greenway Avenue. Streetcars once ran uphill on Greenway to an amusement park at Council Crest. The sidewalk attached to the road bed is wooden. According to Steve Yates, an engineer with the city, it would not be replaced today with wood. This sidewalk is slippery when wet, even in the absence of leaves.

A nice tour of the area's wooden stairs and sidewalks starts at

This wooden staircase, one of the last in town, leads from SW Montgomery Drive to Greenway Avenue.

the Montgomery to Greenway steps. At the top, on Greenway, turn right. You'll see various wooden steps leading off the wooden sidewalk down to homes on the downhill side of Greenway. These are public stairs, built to provide access to homeowners. At Greenway's overpass of Talbot Road, take 25 steps down to Talbot. Walk west; just on the other side of the overpass, take a flight of 51 wooden stairs across from 2840 down to Montgomery Drive. Near the top of these steps, you can see look to the right to see how the wooden sidewalk hangs off of Greenway. Turn right at Montgomery and walk back to the first set of steps, at 2860 SW Montgomery.

The other wooden sidewalk in town is on the Thurman Street Bridge. Walk down the bridge stairs, and stand under the bridge. You won't have to wait long for a runner to cross the bridge; the sound of their thumping feet on the wooden sidewalk is an interesting urban noise.

More wooden steps are the SW Broadway Drive steps to Hoffman, steps at NW 28th Place and Wardway, and in Linnton, steps from the elevated sidewalk along Highway 30 that lead up to 9450 NW Roseway.

The Grand Staircase at Lewis and Clark College

In the hills of Southwest Portland is one of the most beautiful homes of the estate era, before the Great Depression put a stop to extravagance.

In the 1920s, Meier and Frank executive and heir M. Lloyd Frank commissioned architect Herman Brookman to design a 35-room Tudor mansion and estate gardens. The result, Fir Acres, is today the nucleus of Lewis and Clark College. Behind the home, formal gardens stairstep down an east-facing hillside,

A detail of the Frank home's exterior, on the campus of Lewis and Clark College.

with Mount Hood in the exact middle of the view. The home and gardens, while formal, are artistically exuberant; stately, but friendly. A visit on a day bright with fall foliage will create a memory to treasure over a dark winter.

From the back of the home, 83 stone steps descend the hill through a series of terraces, passing a reflecting pond, swimming pool, patios, and wide green lawns. Pick a day when Mount Hood is out.

The gardens and staircase are on the campus of Lewis and Clark College, but are open to the public. They are located at 0615 SW Palatine Hill Road.

Vestigia around Stairs

Stair hunting is not just about the stairs. While the staircases themselves are vestiges of a pedestrian culture, the neighborhoods they're in also have their own stories. Here are two places where what I call vestigia, or traces of our past, are hiding in plain sight.

- SW 10th Avenue dead-end at Clifton. At the base of this 57-step wooden staircase is an old and scenic reservoir pump house made of brick. Before Portland began tapping Bull Run water in 1895, it relied on the Willamette River and on hillside streams and springs, one of which was dammed in this area.

- SW Arthur dead-end east of Naito Parkway. Here is a staircase to a subterranean pedestrian walkway under SW Kelly Avenue. It's a refuge for homeless people especially in bad weather, and is itself a vestige of an era, mid-twentieth

The lid of a submerged garbage can, a means of storing a family's weekly generation of garbage that would be untenable for many homeowners today.

century, when walkers were the last thing on the minds of city planners.

The other bit of vestigia here is set into the driveway of the last house on Arthur. It's an in-ground garbage can, the kind seen in urban neighborhoods where space is limited (such as Alameda Ridge). Lift the lid, and a small metal can could be lifted out and its contents dumped. Its tiny size offers a rebuke from the past to our over-consuming ways today, where most families have not only a 32-gallon garbage can but a huge recycling bin as well.

The View from the Parking Garage

Fear of earthquakes and having to queue up on one of those spiraling exit ramps keep me out of parking garages. But they do have one great aspect: outdoor staircases that provide excellent bird's-eye views of city rooftops and treescapes. My favorite view is from a downtown parking garage in the block bounded by SW 3rd, 4th, Morrison, and Alder.

The southwest corner of the garage (4th and Morrison) is best. Forty-one steps lead to the third floor where views are pretty good; keep going up, 16 steps per floor, and you'll be rewarded

The view from the parking garage, SW 4th and Morrison in downtown Portland.

by views of Pioneer Courthouse's round cupola (1875); the pyramidal glass atrium roof of Pioneer Place (1990); and the red-roofed Pacific Building (1926) which displaced the last cow who grazed in Portland's downtown. South of the Pacific Building is the Hilton Executive Tower; its rows of windows mimic the Pacific's Chicago-style window treatment. Beyond the Pacific is Jackson Tower with its clock (1912), one of Portland's many white terra cotta buildings. And beyond Jackson Tower is the 27-story Fox Tower (2000); its glassy façade reflects Portland's cloudscape in a beautiful way.

This garage's steps end at a ninth-floor rooftop for a total of 137 steps.

North Portland: Stair Poor Except for . . .

adidas America's campus.

▪▪ ▪▪ ▪▪

North Portland is flat relative to the land west of the Willamette River. The land consists of ancient flood deposits and any slopes it has relate to the weathering and erosion of these deposits as the land drains toward either the Willamette or Columbia rivers. Along the Willamette River are bluffs that would make a great backdrop for many urban stairs, and one is planned for the bluff along Willamette Boulevard, near the University of Portland, to connect the residential uplands with Swan Island.

The only stairs along the Willamette River bluff (besides the N Going Street steps) as of early 2010 are along N Greeley Avenue in the Overlook neighborhood, on adidas America's campus. It's an 11-acre site that was once occupied by the Bess Kaiser

One of many staircases leading to brightly colored buildings on the adidas campus on a North Portland bluff.

Hospital. The hospital buildings are intact, on Greeley's west side. Where patients once parked, adidas built colorful new structures, playing fields and courts, and paths and stairs to connect its campus to the rest of Overlook. Its aim was not an enclave but a community asset. South of the campus is Madrona Park, a small Portland park.

Stairs are located:

- Dead-end of Alberta at Delaware up to the campus: 18 steps.

- Dead-end of Humboldt passing downhill through the campus: 58 steps.

- Greeley Avenue up to the campus: 3 staircases.

From the campus, you can walk south on Greeley's west side to a staircase of 77 steps down to N Going Street, a road elevated above railroad lines (good train watching) that leads to a great beach on Swan Island's west shore. Getting there is a bit of a noisy, unpleasant walk, but the riverside park and views are worth it.

A STAIR BY ANY OTHER NAME

The Indo-European root for *stair* is *steigh* from the Old English *stigan*—to go up. The word stirrup sprang from this same root, according to *The American Heritage Dictionary*. And the Irish word *staighre* hasn't grown too far away either.

The Oxford English Dictionary gives some other evocative foreign words for stairs. In Dutch, stair or stairs are, variously: *trap, opstap, tree, trede, treeplank*. *Trede* surely must be a distant cousin to the tread we speak of in English. And *opstap* sounds like a marching order from a drill sergeant.

In German, stair is *treppe*. In Swedish, *trappa*.

The Romance languages inspired the word *escalator*. A moving stairway, the escalator was a trademarked name in 1900. In Spain, *la escalera* leads people upward. In Italy, *la scala* is a stair. In France, you ascend an *escalier*.

A stair dancer, according to *The Oxford English Dictionary*, is a thief who steals from open (unlocked) buildings such as offices.

Dreams about stairs are universal. According to some, dreaming of ascending a flight of stairs means you are achieving a higher level of understanding, and are progressing on your spiritual, emotional, or material journey. A descent, on the other hand, means you will face many setbacks in your endeavors.

From a top flight of the Multnomah County Library steps looking down through the levels.

Public Spaces, Grand Staircases:
Four Fabulous Indoor Stairways

SOME OF PORTLAND'S most interesting staircases are indoors. Featured here are four of them, and they could all be visited on one excursion to downtown and the Pearl District.

Start at the southernmost staircase, located at Portland City Hall, then walk north to the Pioneer Courthouse, west to the Multnomah County Library, and north to the Gerding Theater. Each of these buildings has been restored in the last few decades; wandering through them and the many intriguing places you'll discover along the way makes for a grand day on the town.

Portland City Hall

Portland's City Hall was constructed in 1895 and renovated in 1998. Besides bringing the building up to code, the renovation restored many original features, such as two light wells that bring daylight into interior spaces; they had been closed to create storage and office space in the 1930s. The 4th Avenue main entrance was restored to its original beauty and purpose. (It had been used as a parking lot and the entrance moved to 5th Avenue.) During the restoration, three-fourths of the original marble floor tiles were saved and reinstalled.

Two interior staircases flank the two light wells. Their filigreed plated cast-iron balustrades, cast bronze risers, and marble

On the second floor of Portland City Hall.

treads are original. In 1910, elevators were added next to them. The stairs ascend to the fourth floor, for a total of 77 steps. While on the steps you can look across the light wells into windows where the "City that Works" is working, for a literal example of government transparency.

Notice the saffron-colored columns around the stairs. Though they look like marble, they are actually plaster decorated in a technique called *scagliola*. In it, pigmented plaster is the base; veining is created by drawing strands of raw silk saturated in other pigments through the wet plaster; other layers of pigment can be troweled on and then cut back to resemble natural color variation in stone. When dry the surface is pumiced smooth then buffed with oiled felt; beeswax is sometimes used as a finishing agent. The labor involved would make this process far more expensive today than simply using marble itself.

City Hall (1221 SW 4th Avenue) is open Monday through Friday. Its rooms, including the splendid Council Chambers, can be rented. Call the Bureau of General Services for information: 503-823-5252.

The Pioneer Courthouse

Inside Pioneer Courthouse in downtown Portland, the twenty-first century fades. Built beginning in 1869, and completed in 1875, it is still a working courthouse, one of four primary locations where the United States Court of Appeals for the Ninth Circuit hears oral arguments. It also houses the chambers (offices) of Portland-based judges of the Ninth Circuit. When it was built, it was far from the city, and was criticized for its remoteness. Now it is next door to Pioneer Courthouse Square, which has come to be known as Portland's living room.

The fifth-floor cupola at the 1875 Pioneer Courthouse. Downtown buildings shimmer slightly through the windows' wavy old glass.

The old wooden staircases—with ornate wooden balustrades between the first and fourth floors and period wool carpets covering the treads—are beautiful. Also wondrous is a nineteenth-century, paneled courtroom with a fireplace on the second floor. It's an active courtroom, so it may not be accessible at all times.

Most spectacular and rewarding for stair-climbers is the glassed-in cupola, a one-room fifth floor, accessible only by stair, at the rooftop level. Inside, it's like being in an urban tree house, with 360-degree views of downtown Portland. A few chairs, a table, and some Portland-related reading materials make this a nice respite from downtown's busyness. On all the floors are historic Portland photographs and interpretive displays.

The stair count: 9 steps outside to the front door; 30 to the second floor; 26 to the third floor; 18 to the fourth floor; and 32 to the cupola, for a total of 115.

The courthouse is at 555 SW Yamhill. Access it on the 6th Avenue side. It is open to visitors Monday through Friday, except for national holidays. Be prepared to pass through security and provide photo identification.

Multnomah County Library

The Central Library of the Multnomah County Library System was designed by A. E. Doyle and opened in 1913. By 1994, structural problems were apparent, and the library closed for significant rebuilding and renovation. When it reopened in 1997, one element caused a stir: a new, 16-step, black granite flight of stairs. Artist Larry Kirkland sandblasted garden-themed art and words into the stairs' treads and risers, as part of the library's theme of "A Garden of Knowledge." Above the first grand flight are 16 more steps to the second floor, also black granite; their treads are incised with the Greek key motif. These 32 granite stairs replaced marble steps that had worn out.

The marble stairs from the second to third floors are original; there are 44 of them, for a total of 76 steps.

Kirkland also worked with architects Fletcher Farr Ayotte to weave the garden motif into other aspects of the building such as a garland in the foyer ceiling, and carpet patterns of roses and leaves. Other artists picked up the theme as well: the bark of a bronze tree in the Children's Library combines elements of Oregon's natural history with subjects found in the Dewey decimal

The first 16 steps at the Multnomah County Library. Figures of dogs, squirrels, sports equipment, and even a compass (of the sort used in geometry class) are incised into the steps. It's fun to slow down and discover what figures and words are hiding among the swirling leaves and flowers.

system. The large vase of fresh flowers at the top of the first landing is a tradition revived with the renovation.

The library is at SW 10th and Yamhill. It is open daily; call 503-988-5123 for hours of operation.

Gerding Theater at the Armory

The 25 steps of the Joanne Lilley Grand Staircase are housed in a former National Guard Armory in the Pearl District. When the Armory was built in 1891, the surrounding area was residential, with churches and schools, though it soon transitioned

The dramatic Joanne Lilley Grand Staircase inside the once-cavernous Armory, now home to Portland Center Stage.

into a warehouse and factory district. While soldiers mustered at the Armory in 1898 for the Spanish American War, no urban unrest was ever quelled here. In 1968, after years as an event space, it became a beer warehouse, owned by Blitz Weinhard Brewery.

In 1999, the building was purchased by Gerding Edlen as part of the redevelopment of the Brewery Blocks, former factories and warehouses long occupied by Blitz Weinhard.

In 2006, the renovated building became the Gerding Theater at the Armory, home to Portland Center Stage, a large regional theater company. Naming opportunities were presented to theater patrons and to the public to help retire the debt incurred during the renovation. For $1,891, a chair would be named in your honor (the price reflects the year the building was constructed). Joanne Lilley, a charter producer of Portland Center Stage, donated $500,000 and the staircase was named for her.

The steps are cantilevered off a second-floor balcony. Everything in this building is new; from its construction in 1891 until the 2006 renovation, there was nothing inside but space under the vaulting roof trusses.

The Armory is at 128 NW 11th Avenue and is open daily. Call 503-445-3700 or visit www.pcs.org.

SEEN AND HEARD ON THE STEPS

On the hundreds of staircases I walked for this book, I saw numerous cats, one rat, many sweaty people running staircases repeatedly in both directions, and, especially on Alameda Ridge, countless morning walkers whose chatty voices wafted up staircases ahead of them, betraying no huffing and puffing. Locals, for sure.

One day while camped on a staircase so I could talk to some stair-climbers, I heard someone coming: it was a woman talking real estate on her cell phone as she descended. "It always makes you feel good once the papers are signed," she said with compassion. She didn't even see me, though. Her tiny black

Bella the Cat insisted on a petting on the NW Vaughn Street steps in Willamette Heights.

poodle and I looked at each other sympathetically, both hoping for a little attention.

Homeowners seem to look somewhat fondly, if sometimes with exasperation, upon living next to a staircase. One man at the top of some steps off Cornell Road said, "We have company on them sometimes," which seemed a very nice euphemism for rowdy beer drinkers. He and his partner pick up the cans on their way to dinner on NW 23rd Avenue. On Alameda Ridge, one mom told me she gets after the teens who party on the steps outside her window. Her tone was maternalistic, expressing the fact that "kids will be kids."

Public stairs have lives of their own, and the best way to get to know one, absent living next to it, is to plunk down with a book and keep your ears and eyes open.

On the Stair Trail:
Five Stairway Treks

THE FIVE URBAN excursions in this section cover about fifty staircases in Portland's most stair-rich neighborhoods, and vary from 3.5 to 5.25 miles. There are two excursions in Southwest Portland, where stairs abound, and one each in Northwest, Southeast, and Northeast. My goals were to create new routes through what may be to some people familiar territory, to visit the maximum number of staircases in a reasonable walk length, and to pass by or near food, drink, or shops. After all, these routes are in the city, and one of the best parts of a city walk is hanging out in a different neighborhood for a while.

Public restrooms are scarce on some routes, so buying something at a commercial establishment along the way and using its facilities may be the best option.

- Southwest: River to Heights

- Outer Southwest: Peaks and Valleys

- Northwest: Nob Hill and Westover

- Southeast: Mount Tabor Neighborhood and Park

- Northeast: Alameda Ridge

A spectacular Japanese maple creates a canopy on a 131-step staircase in the Hillside neighborhood.

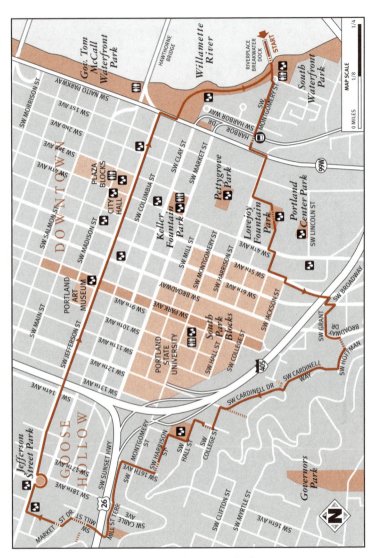

River to Heights Stair Climb

SOUTHWEST: *River to Heights Stair Climb*

DISTANCE
3.5 miles

TOTAL STEPS
631: 328 ascending, 303 descending

STARTING POINT
East of SW Montgomery Street in South Waterfront Park, atop
a floating Willamette River dock

TRANSIT AND PARKING
TriMet: see www.trimet.org for the various buses that stop near
RiverPlace. Then walk to Montgomery's end at the river.

The nearest metered parking is a lot with five-hour spaces
on Naito Parkway, south of Market Street. Enter northbound
only; carpools only Monday through Friday, 6 a.m. to 10 a.m.
There are for-fee garages in the RiverPlace area.

NEARBY COMMERCIAL AREAS
At the beginning, along the river are shops and restaurants at
RiverPlace. About midway, along SW Jefferson Street in Goose
Hollow, are fast-food places, coffee shops, and a few restaurants.

PUBLIC RESTROOMS
At the start: SW Montgomery at South Waterfront Park

✳ This stair trail is noisy but rich in the juxtapositions of beauty and decay that make for an excellent city walk. The transition zone between the heights and the flats combines isolation, interesting architecture, and distant views. Some staircases, enshrouded by greenery, feel remote; walk with a partner if you are concerned.

❖ **BEGIN** east of SW Montgomery Street in South Waterfront Park, atop a floating Willamette River dock (beyond the floating restaurant). Portland Parks manages the dock, issuing permits for overnight visitors.

↗ From the dock, ascend a ramp and **9** steps. Watch for bikes and turn right at the sidewalk. At a traffic circle, head west on Montgomery.

↗ Cross Harbor Way and Harbor Drive and climb **57** steps at Montgomery's dead-end. At the second landing, to the right is the home of Portland Park Rangers, who keep city parks safe, issue permits, and ensure that no one's dog is drinking off-leash.

At the top of the stairs, turn left, walk to Harrison, and turn right. After 1st Avenue, turn left at a crosswalk onto a pedestrian walkway. Since the 1960s, 2nd Avenue has seen only foot traffic here in Portland's first urban renewal area.

↗ On the right the Lovejoy Fountain's terraces mimic erosion in Oregon's deserts. Climb **25** steps or so to the fountain's southwest corner. Carefully cross another pedestrian walkway (the old 3rd Avenue) and head to a sculpture on 4th Avenue.

Turn left at 4th and right at College Street, passing an old sycamore in a parking lot. It and a few homes are vestiges of the neighborhood here from the 1870s until the 1960s.

Turn left at 5th. At Jackson, cross to 5th's west side. Veer right after crossing over Interstate 405; turn right on Broadway, cross 6th and cross Broadway again; turn right and climb a hill to SW Grant Street, a refuge after that stressful bit of roadway. Homes at 620, 634, 638, and 642 date from 1880.

↗ Grant ends at Broadway Drive. Turn left. Soon, across from an alley, is a wooden staircase set against a cliff. Cross carefully to it. These **203** steps are divided by 13 landings. They are isolated, a bit creepy, and delightful. At the top, turn right on Hoffman. Walk to a path at road's end, cross a small ravine and emerge onto Cardinell Way. Homes are built on stilts. Great views abound.

Pass through a gate and turn right onto Cardinell Drive. Pass a wooden staircase leading to a brick remnant from an old reservoir. Interstate 405 roars loudly here; homes from the 1920s were erected when the noise level was far lower.

↘ Take the left, higher level of College, which is split in two. Climb steeply. Descend **69** steps and continue straight on 13th. It curves left and becomes Hall Street.

↗ Turn right at 14th and left at Harrison, which offers more great old homes. At 1501 is a spectacular Italianate residence. It was built in 1882 by Morris Marks, a shoe merchant who had emigrated from Poland. The home was moved to this site in 1910 from its original location at the southwest corner of SW 11th and Clay. Veer left and climb **34** wooden stairs to 16th, a street where residents have improvised devices to keep themselves from sliding downhill.

Walk downhill on 16th, carefully crossing Montgomery to 16th's dead-end at a multi-use path. Watch for bikes, then turn left onto it. Ahead are the tunnels for Highway 26.

Beyond 18th, the path becomes Mill Street Terrace; above, a cable railway in the 1890s carried people to Portland Heights. Pass Cable Avenue, worth a look, and climb as Mill heads over the tunnels and dead-ends.

↘↘ Descend **152** steps here. At the bottom, Market Street Drive, turn left (yes, uphill, but just a bit!) and right to descend **82** steps across from 1952. At the bottom are two rewards: an 1871 mansion and a heritage Blue Atlas cedar.

Walk to Jefferson, planked in 1851 to make it easier for Tualatin Valley farmers to traverse a muddy pass through the West Hills. At the MAX stop, wood plank benches evoke that history. Turn right and stay on Jefferson to the river and pass a truly fabulous cornucopia of architectural styles and eras, with old homes, streetcar-era apartments, an elm-lined park, elegant churches, significant buildings (the Portland Art Museum and

City Hall, to name a few), and mid-twentieth century offices in the egregious but now-historic Brutalist style.

At Jefferson and Naito Parkway, turn right, walk one block to Columbia, turn left and enter Waterfront Park. Walk right (south) to the start. ■

In the 1950s the 1871 Kamm Mansion was moved to SW 20th Avenue from its original home to make way for construction of Lincoln High, at SW Salmon and 14th. A few heritage trees remain on the campus from that earlier era.

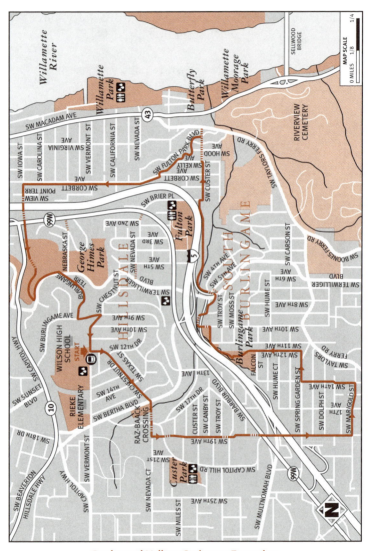

Peaks and Valleys Staircase Excursion

OUTER SOUTHWEST: *Peaks and Valleys Staircase Excursion*

DISTANCE
5.25 miles

TOTAL STEPS
531: 279 ascending, 252 descending (450 feet of net elevation gain)

STARTING POINT
SW Vermont Street and Chestnut Drive

TRANSIT AND PARKING
TriMet: bus 1 stops at SW Vermont and Chestnut Drive, though this bus only runs during rush hour on weekdays.

Street parking is available but watch for restrictions based on events and school hours at nearby Wilson High.

NEARBY COMMERCIAL AREAS
About two-thirds of the way through the route, at SW Macadam and Taylors Ferry Road, is Zupan's Market. At the end, north of Wilson High School is the Hillsdale Shopping Center at SW Sunset Boulevard and Capitol Highway. In it are great options for shopping, restaurants, and coffee, as well as a grocery store.

PUBLIC RESTROOMS
None

✳ This walk explores peaks and valleys in sidewalk-challenged Southwest Portland, where the steep and uneven landscape has resulted in the occasional road platted but never built and once-unvisited greenspaces adjacent to busy arterials. Along the route, note the many signs for SW Trails, a group created by Southwest resident Don Baack and others. Since 1996, they've opened unused rights-of-way and built on-grade stairs out of wood and gravel to create back-door links to Southwest's many geographically separated neighborhoods.

This walk traverses isolated areas. Bring a friend if you feel unsafe walking alone.

❖ **BEGIN** at SW Vermont and Chestnut Drive. Walk Chestnut downhill to Bertha Boulevard. Cross it and enter a 3.3-acre natural area, where year-round Stephens Creek meets Custer Creek on their way to the Willamette River.

↘↗ Walk down **26** steps, over wetlands on a boardwalk, and up **39** steps out of the valley, on a trail blazed as a safe school route in the 1960s by Werner Raz. By the 1990s it was overgrown; in 2007, Don Baack and other SW Trails volunteers rebuilt it and it's now called the Raz-Baack Crossing.

↗ Cross Capitol Hill Road; climb **10** steps and follow a dirt path to a meadow, once pasture for dairy cattle (as was Wilson High). Keep far left, watching for a narrow opening in the greenery: the 19th Avenue right-of-way. Turn left at it; it leads to Capitol Hill Road; cross the road, aiming for a fire hydrant on the other side. (If you miss the narrow opening in the green-

Don Baack at the Raz-Baack Crossing built by SWTrails in 2007. The stairs were built for less than $100 with 325 hours of volunteer labor.

ery, walk on graveled Nevada Street, turn left at 21st, and left at Capitol Hill Road to rejoin the route.)

↗ ↘ ↗ Stay on 19th as its personality alternates from asphalt to rutted path, and it climbs and descends a 550-foot-high peak. Along the way, you'll climb **4** steps, descend **6**, and ascend **34** to Barbur Boulevard and Capitol Hill Road.

Cross Barbur, jog a hair to the right and stay on 19th, crossing Interstate 5 on a lovely old bridge. Turn left at Marigold. At

17th, next to a 1926 community hall that hosts ballroom dancing, enter a Water Bureau HydroPark. Walk a deeply wooded path, emerge on Marigold at 15th, and then turn left at 14th.

↗↘ From 14th, turn right at Spring Garden; cross it carefully, veer left at a fork toward 12th and follow 12th several scenic blocks. At Falcon, jog left to an asphalt path at Burlingame Park, 4.6 acres acquired in 1949, just before the freeway altered the atmosphere here. Pass tennis courts and enter a forest. Exit it at Canby and 11th. Stay straight on Canby; go left at 10th. Climb **3** steps into a greenspace and descend **55** steps. Exit the greenspace at a dead-end of 4th Avenue.

↘ On 4th, pass under Terwilliger. On the left a gravel path leads into the no-man's-land alongside Interstate 5. Take it, descend **65** steps, then turn right on a service road that leads to a dead-end of Custer Street. At Brier Place, turn right; a quick left puts you back on Custer. Follow it downhill, and nod to Mount Hood, dead ahead. At Corbett, the view is sublime.

↘↗ At Custer and Kelly, stair fun begins again. Descend a **100**-step staircase broken by sidewalks and streets. At the bottom of the Custer steps, turn around and climb **60** steps back to Fulton Park Boulevard. You've begun the return leg.

Walk uphill on Fulton Park Boulevard; turn right on Corbett. Stay on its west side, and left when it splits in two levels, to gain outstanding views of the Willamette River, Ross Island, and downtown.

↗ At Iowa turn left. Walk beyond View Point Terrace and enter a

The balustrades on two staircases up to a Terwilliger Boulevard overpass and ramp at the intersection of SW 4th and SW 5th avenues have the distinctive green paint and design often used on Portland's public stairs.

greenspace that links with 32-acre George Himes Park. Climb a total of **129** steps, treading far below Interstate 5 and Barbur. At a fork in the trail, just past the last steps, turn right and hike uphill. At the top of the park, at Terwilliger, go left onto the asphalt multi-use trail.

From Terwilliger, turn right at Burlingame Terrace, left on Burlingame Avenue, and right on Chestnut. At 10th, Chestnut becomes Vermont. Follow it to the starting point. ∎

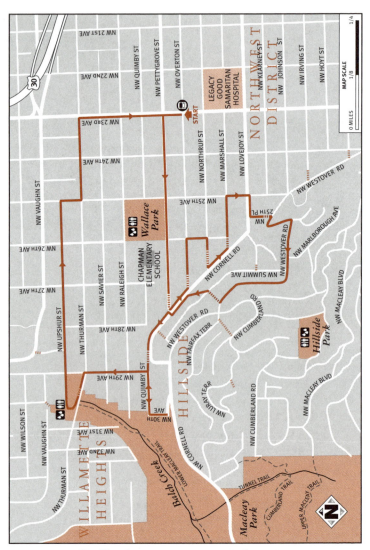

Nob Hill and Westover Streetcar Stairway Jaunt

NORTHWEST: *Nob Hill and Westover Streetcar Stairway Jaunt*

DISTANCE
3.5 miles

TOTAL STEPS
533: 169 ascending, 364 descending

STARTING POINT
NW 23rd Avenue and Overton Street

TRANSIT AND PARKING
TriMet: bus 15 stops at NW 23rd and Overton. It runs seven days a week, with frequent service at rush hour. The Portland Streetcar stops nearby, at NW 23rd and Marshall, two blocks south of the starting point.

Park on city streets or in for-fee lots along NW 23rd Avenue. Be aware that street parking is challenging here.

NEARBY COMMERCIAL AREAS
NW 23rd Avenue from Burnside to Thurman, and NW Thurman west of 23rd (near the walk's end) are both full of places to eat, drink, shop, and read.

PUBLIC RESTROOMS
At Wallace Park, NW 25th and Raleigh, a few blocks from the stair trail's starting point.
Multnomah County Library's Northwest branch, when open: NW 23rd and Thurman

✱ Most of the staircases on this route enabled residents of hillside neighborhoods in the early 1900s to access streetcar lines. One line ran on 23rd south to Council Crest. Its tracks, paved over repeatedly since the line was abandoned in 1950, reappeared in potholes each winter. In 2010, they were pulled up in a major street repair project. Along Pettygrove, west of 25th, look for streetcar tracks appearing here and there in the street. Gorgeous homes provide plenty of excuses to stop, and one of the steepest staircases in town will challenge your knees. Near the end, the walk drops into Balch Creek Canyon, portal to Forest Park and the beautiful Lower Macleay Trail along Balch Creek.

⬛ ⬛ ⬛

↗ From NW 23rd and Overton, walk one block north and turn left on Pettygrove. Across from the last two homes on Pettygrove, climb **65** steps. At the top, turn left on Cornell Road. Once a Native American route through the hills, in the 1840s it became known as Balch Road, for Danforth Balch, who homesteaded in the canyon near the walk's end. Some time after Balch was hanged for gunning down his son-in-law, the road's name changed.

↘ Past 2701 NW Cornell, descend one of the prettiest staircases in town, **56** steps with a curving sidewalk between flights. It ends at Overton's dead-end.

↗ Walk east on Overton, turn right on 26th, and right on Northrup. The street ends in one block and you might think you're in San Francisco. A sidewalk cleaves this **63**-step staircase midway between flights; a home shares this hidden space with a large horsechestnut. At the top, you're again on Cornell. Turn left.

↘ At a bus stop, take **55** steps to 26th and Marshall. Walk east on Marshall, slowly; among many fascinating buildings on this block is Arenson Court, a 1930 brick apartment building, now condominiums. Like many of Portland's 1920s-era apartments, it was designed by Elmer Feig, who never passed up a chance to add a bit of charm to his work.

Commuter steps leading up from the dead-end of NW Northrup Street to Cornell Road.

↗ From Marshall, turn right on 25th. Cross Lovejoy, turn right on it, and then left on 25th Place, which ends at a debutante-worthy staircase of **41** steps to Westover Road. At Westover, turn right and climb.

At 2560, Westover takes a sharp turn. At Westover Circle is the site of Saint Vincent Hospital from 1895 to 1971. Cross Marlborough and Summit; homes enjoy city views and walkers enjoy views of the homes.

↘ Past 2763 is a show-off of a staircase, long, steep, and visually daunting. Benches hidden on landings are ignored by runners. Near the bottom of its **157** steps, note the rain gutter in the railing, and carefully turn left on Summit Avenue. Keep right at the fork, Summit Court.

From Summit Court, turn left on Cornell. Cross to its north side at the crosswalk and walk uphill.

↘ The Cornell sidewalk ends at 2865; continue to **25** steps hidden on the right. They lead to one of the most beautiful blocks in town, NW Quimby between 29th and 30th. At the bottom of the steps, walk west on Quimby to explore this block.

At 30th turn left. It ends at an older alignment of Cornell. On the corner, limbs of a stupendous Japanese pagoda tree defy gravity. From it, retrace your steps to Quimby and 29th.

Walk north on 29th; the next three blocks are one steep, straight stretch of road. Cross Raleigh and Savier. Both dead-end at Balch Creek Canyon.

A bench on the 157-step Summit to Westover steps invites climbers to rest before the final two flights. Note the absence of moss on these much-used steps.

↘ While on 29th, cross Thurman and then turn left on it; walk to the Thurman Street Bridge which has spanned the canyon since 1903. At the bridge's northeast end, take **71** steps down to a portal into 5,000-acre Forest Park. To the left, a good detour is the Lower Macleay Trail. In less than a quarter mile you can walk along deeply forested Balch Creek. (The creek flows underground in its final mile but runs wild upstream of the bridge.)

From the stairs, turn right and exit the park via a vehicle turn-around. Walk east on quiet Upshur. At 28th, on the left once sat the 1904 Forestry Center, possibly the world's largest log cabin. It burned in 1964. At 26th, apartments were built as the Fairmount Hotel for Portland's 1905 Lewis and Clark Exposition, a world's fair. The fair entrance was at 26th and Upshur; beyond, fairgrounds spread north and west, in what is now the Guilds Lake Industrial Sanctuary.

From Upshur turn right on 25th and left on Thurman. Look for a tree swallowing a fire hydrant. From here on, extend your walk with coffee, books, food, or shopping. At 23rd and Thurman turn south (right) and return to the start. ■

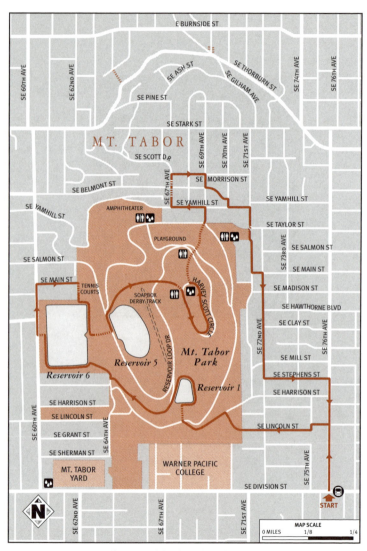

Mount Tabor Neighborhood and Park Stair Walk

SOUTHEAST: *Mount Tabor Neighborhood and Park Stair Walk*

DISTANCE
4 miles

TOTAL STEPS
628: 270 ascending, 358 descending (about 400 feet of net elevation gain)

STARTING POINT
SE 76th Avenue and Division Street

TRANSIT AND PARKING
TriMet: bus 4 stops at SE 76th Avenue and Division Street. It runs seven days a week with frequent service during rush hour.

Parking is available along SE 76th Avenue.

NEARBY COMMERCIAL AREAS
At SE 60th and Division and SE 60th and Stark

PUBLIC RESTROOMS
At the summit of Mount Tabor is a portable toilet. Downhill to the northwest of the summit is a playground, and just downhill of it are year-round restrooms.

✳ Mount Tabor, a 640-foot peak that erupts from Portland's relatively flat east side, is treasured by Portlanders, and for good reason. With forests, vistas, and historic open-air reservoirs, it is a visual feast. This route explores the park and a few of the streets sited scenically on its flanks. Homes are varied and offer fans of architecture plenty to enjoy. Cars are not allowed in the park on Wednesdays.

❖ **BEGIN** at SE 76th and Division. Walk north on 76th and turn left at Lincoln. Continue on Lincoln as it jogs at 75th. Enter Mount Tabor Park at Lincoln's dead-end, past 72nd.

↗ Head uphill, through a playground and under big trees, to a road. Turn left on it. Continue to **81** steps on the right. At the top is Reservoir 1, built in 1894 in a small ravine. It holds 12 million gallons of water. Turn right on the path and walk around the reservoir. A freeform public alter sits at the north end on remnants of a long-ago drinking fountain.

At the reservoir's southwest corner, take the downhill paved road with an iron railing along it. Ignore side trails and enjoy great southwest views. At a T in the road, turn right.

↘ Ahead is Reservoir 6, which holds 31.9 million gallons in each of its halves. Keep left, to the reservoir's south side; follow around to its west side and descend **43** steps to SE 60th Avenue.

↘ Turn right on 60th and right on Main, a gorgeous street. At its dead-end, re-enter the park, taking a sharp right down **12** earthen steps, then walking along the west side of tennis courts. At Reservoir 6, turn left to walk around it.

Reservoir 1 on Mount Tabor is one of five open-air reservoirs in Portland holding treated water that ultimately flows to Portland's west side, a set-up scheduled to end by around 2014 to comply with EPA regulations. The gatehouse is made of concrete, hammered and tooled to look like stone building blocks.

↗ From the reservoir's east side, climb **134** steps, including a severe, **96**-step section with no landings and steep risers. At the top is Reservoir 5, which holds 49 million gallons. Go left.

At the reservoir's northwest corner, take a gravel path diagonally uphill. Where the path forks, go right (uphill) through a beautiful stand of Douglas fir. At one point on the right is a narrow, straight bit of roadway. It's a soapbox derby track.

At a paved road, Reservoir Loop Drive, either turn left onto it for a longer but more leisurely stroll to the summit, or cross the road to continue on the path, which gets very steep here.

↗ The path ends at an old brick restroom. Climb a final **12** steps to Harvey Scott Circle, the summit loop road, well worth a stroll around. The summit is the grassy area within the loop.

↘ From the north end of the loop road, begin a descent of Mount Tabor's epic, **282**-step staircase. Descend **18** steps to a path that leads to a series of stairs heading downhill. On the left is the cap of subterranean Reservoir 7; it was built in 1912. The staircase, broken by landings, sidewalks, and roads, is rarely empty; as I descended, I encountered a sweaty, straggling parade of runners, all going up, and most looking pained, but with the reward of virtue and endorphins awaiting at the summit. To truly be a local, I'd advise you turn around at the bottom and go back up.

↘↗ At the bottom, walk straight onto 69th, and left on Yamhill, a beautiful street that hugs the park's north boundary. Turn right at 67th and after a bit, descend **21** steps on the right to Belmont Street. Cross it carefully and climb **18** steps that lead to a gravel path. It ends at Scott Drive and Morrison Street.

Turn right on Morrison and right on 69th. At Belmont turn left onto gravel, Belmont's final block. At 70th, turn right then left onto Yamhill.

↗ From Yamhill, turn right on 71st. At Taylor and 71st, climb **25** steps into the park. Stay left on a dirt path that leads to the dead-end of 71st.

From 71st turn left on Main, right on 72nd, left on Stephens, and right on 76th to return to the start. ∎

A corduroy ribbon of stairs, some of the 282 steps that lead to the summit of
Mount Tabor.

Alameda Ridge Stair Circuit

NORTHEAST: *Alameda Ridge Stair Circuit*

DISTANCE
5 miles

TOTAL STEPS
805 (or 1,436 counting ascents and descents of the same staircase)

STARTING POINT
The Sabin HydroPark, NE 19th Avenue and Prescott Street

TRANSIT AND PARKING
TriMet: bus 8 stops at NE 15th and Prescott; from there, walk four blocks east to the start. The bus runs seven days a week with frequent service at rush hour.

Parking is available along streets adjacent to the starting point.

NEARBY COMMERCIAL AREAS
At NE Fremont and 15th is a grocery store, coffee shop, and small shops and restaurants. At NE 24th and Fremont are more shops and restaurants. At the stair trail's halfway point, NE 50th and Sandy Boulevard, is a Northeast Portland icon: the Rheinlander and Gustav's Bier Stube. Sandy Boulevard is lined with other restaurants in that area.

PUBLIC RESTROOMS
None

✳ This first half of this eleven-staircase walk stays low, heading southeast along the base of four-mile-long Alameda Ridge, and offers the chance to tread every staircase that seams this granite-filled relic of the Missoula Floods. On the return leg, the walk traverses the ridge top. Along the way, century-old homes, from cottages to mansions, will delight and entertain you with their general impeccability and considerable charm.

❖ **BEGIN** at the Sabin HydroPark, NE 19th and Prescott. It's a small urban park created out of formerly fenced-off Portland Water Bureau land. Walk through it to 19th and Skidmore, passing the Sabin Community Garden. Walk south on 19th.

↘ At 19th's dead-end, descend a **51**-step staircase. Continue on 19th, passing one end of Alameda, which morphs into the less sinuous Shaver Street west of here.

↗↘ Turn left onto Ridgewood Drive; walk this lovely street to a staircase just past 24th. Climb and descend its **75** steps.

↗↘ Back on Ridgewood, turn left at the bottom of the staircase; cross 25th. At a wide intersection, turn left at Stuart Drive. There are **70** steps on the right, past the first house. Climb, look around, and come down.

At the base of the Stuart stairs, turn left; rejoin Ridgewood, heading east; cross Regents Drive, keeping on Ridgewood (not on 26th). At 29th, Ridgewood becomes Edgehill Place.

↗↘ Follow Edgehill to Fremont and turn left. Pass one house on Fremont and turn left onto the steps. Climb **98** of them to Alameda Terrace and come back down.

At the bottom of a 43-step staircase is a dead-end of interesting Craftsman bungalows on NE 50th Avenue. This neighborhood, Rose City Park, was built in the years following the 1905 world's fair.

↗ ↘ Follow Fremont east. Just west of 32nd, climb another set of stairs, **65** steps this time, up to Alameda Terrace. Descend.

From Fremont, turn right on 33rd, where author Beverly Cleary sledded in the 1920s. Cross 33rd at the Klickitat crosswalk, and continue downhill on 33rd.

From 33rd, turn left at Siskiyou. Pass Merges Drive/35th Avenue and stay on curving Siskiyou. At 35th Place, follow Siskiyou as it turns left. At 36th Avenue, turn right and then left onto Morris. At 37th, Morris's name changes to Wistaria Drive.

↗ ↘ From Wistaria turn left at 38th; a **78**-step staircase is across from 3041. Climb to Alameda and descend.

↗ ↘ Continue east on Wistaria. At César E Chávez Boulevard, carefully cross to the southeast corner and continue east. At 42nd is a dangerous intersection. Best to cross 42nd one block south at Stanton and return to the route at the southeast corner of Wistaria and 42nd. The next staircase is at 4131 NE Wistaria. Climb its **127** steps to Alameda and descend.

↗ ↘ Walk not far enough to catch your breath and climb the next **118**-step staircase to Alameda at 4243. Descend it and continue east on Wistaria.

↘ At 47th, cross to Wistaria's south side. Cross 48th; at the narrowing sidewalk, descend **30** steps to lower Wistaria at 49th.

↘ Cross 49th; continue uphill on lower Wistaria. Turn right at stairs that soon appear; **43** steps deliver you to a pretty dead-

A charming home on NE 33rd Place, a street hidden on the edge of Alameda Ridge.

end, NE 50th. Follow it to Sandy Boulevard, where good food will reward you.

↗ From Sandy Boulevard, walk north on 51st. At its dead-end take **50** steps to Wistaria and turn left.

At Alameda, veer slightly left to walk west on it. Continue on Alameda. At 4190, Beaumont intersects on the left; keep right to stay on Alameda. At Siskiyou/42nd, keep left to stay on Alameda. Cross 41st with care.

Leave Alameda by turning left on Klickitat. At 37th stay on Klickitat, then turn right on 35th, left on Beakey, and right on 33rd Place.

At Fremont, turn left. At 33rd Avenue, cross to the northwest corner and walk one block north on 33rd. Turn left onto Alameda.

At 32nd Place/Alameda Terrace, keep straight on Alameda. Cross Alameda Terrace again, then cross Regents Drive and 29th. West of this intersection, take the right fork, Hamblet. At 24th, turn left and then right onto Gile Terrace, a hidden sliver of a street.

Rejoin Alameda at 22nd and turn left onto Alameda. Then turn right on 21st, and left on Alameda Drive. At Mason walk straight on 20th; turn left at Skidmore and right into the HydroPark. ■

STAIR VOCABULARY 101

Each step in a staircase consists of a **tread** and a **riser**. The tread is the part that is stepped on. The riser is the vertical portion between each tread. The riser may be missing, creating a floating, open effect. The majority of Portland's outdoor public stairs have concrete treads and risers. The Elevator Stairs, at SW Broadway Drive to Hoffman Avenue, are some of the relatively few remaining wooden staircases in town. Aluminum stairs, usually without risers, are also used.

A **flight** is a series of steps uninterrupted by a **landing**, which is the area at the top or bottom of a staircase; an intermediate landing is built between flights so the user can rest or so that the staircase can change direction or alignment. The Mount Tabor staircase from Reservoir 6 to Reservoir 5 offers an unusually long flight of 96 steps, untempered by a landing. The French call a landing a *palier de repos* (level of repose). After 96 steps, repose sounds very good. Landings on Portland's outdoor stairs vary from a square bit of concrete traversed in a step or two, to long stretches of sidewalk or unpaved paths, to roadways between flights.

Winders are steps that are narrower on one side than the other, a feature that allows the direction of the stairs to change without a landing. A spiral stairway is a series of winders. One lovely winder is in Linnton at 108th Street and 2nd Avenue.

The **balustrade** is the system of **railings** and **balusters** that prevents people from falling over the edge, rarely an issue with landscape stairs. The railing is also called a **banister** or **hand-**

A decorative balustrade on the Broadway Bridge steps.

The NW Cornell Road to Summit Avenue steps. The treads are leaf-covered in October, scenic but slippery. The landing here is a sidewalk leading to more flights. The gutter on the banister is a rare feature, seen in Portland on just a few other outdoor staircases. Its functionality is debatable; its beauty is not.

rail. Balusters are the vertical pieces that support the banister. In Portland, many staircases have a green balustrade in a vaguely Art Deco style. The spiraling of the balusters at the bottom of a staircase is a **volute**, a feature seen at the base of Multnomah County's Central Library steps on page 73.

Portland's Stairways:
The List

THIS LIST CONTAINS three sections: Portland Street Stairs, Willamette River Bridge Stairs, and Portland Park Stairs. Most of the stairs in the first section are on the City of Portland's list of exterior public staircases, maintained by the Bureau of Transportation. To the city's list I added stairs built by SW Trails, a citizen-led trail-building group that is part of SW Neighborhoods, Inc., and one spectacular staircase in Northwest Portland built by a private developer.

Staircases with fewer than 10 steps are not included unless I deemed them to be of particular scenic interest. Stairs on or connected to public school or university property are not listed, nor are interior public and exterior private stairways. For park stairs, only significant landscape stairs are included. Southwest Portland's Washington Park is the exception. It has more than 20 staircases, many of which are spectacular and definitely significant. While I could have listed them all, that would mean you wouldn't have the fun of finding them yourself!

Counting stairs is not as straightforward as it appears. My counts differ from counts on the city's list. I count the number of risers, which means that the risers that lead to intermediary landings and the top landing are counted as steps. Stairs in a series (for example, separated by sidewalks, roads, gravel, dirt paths, or landings) are listed as one staircase. If flights are sepa-

The view from NW Skyline Boulevard atop a 167-step staircase.

rated by sidewalks, roads, or paths, I don't count the steps taken to traverse those interruptions.

My list of Portland Street Stairs is divided into the city's five geographic divisions. Within each division, staircases are listed in roughly contiguous fashion. Neighborhood designations are courtesy of www.portlandmaps.com and Neighborhood Associations and Neighborhood Coalitions, a neighborhood boundary map produced by the City of Portland. I have appended some historic neighborhood names to these official names.

Each staircase is listed from the bottom location to the top, with a few exceptions, made for access issues, which are worded accordingly. For brevity's sake, I've left off the terms "street" or "avenue" after a road's name unless it is part of the name (Market Street Drive) or where a similarly named street might create confusion. Numbered streets in Portland are always avenues (except in Linnton) unless otherwise noted (such as SE 66th Place). In Portland, named roads (Irving, for example) are generally "streets" unless otherwise noted (such as Burlingame or Water Avenue).

There are 10,155 steps listed in total. The breakdown is:

4,545 Southwest Portland streets and parks
2,167 Northwest Portland streets and parks
  986 Northeast Portland streets and parks
1,134 Southeast Portland streets and parks
  225 North Portland streets and parks
1,098 Bridges

PORTLAND STREET STAIRS

LOCATION	NUMBER OF STEPS	NEIGHBORHOOD
SOUTHWEST		
Montgomery at Harbor Drive to Naito Parkway	57	Downtown
Grant dead-end west of Water to path leading to northbound Naito	29	Downtown
Sherman dead-end west of Water to northbound Naito	12	Downtown
Caruthers dead-end west of Water to northbound Naito	16	Downtown
Arthur dead-end east of Naito: northern steps into pedestrian tunnel under Kelly	19	South Portland
Kelly east of Naito: southern steps to pedestrian tunnel under Kelly	18	South Portland
Kelly, south side to 022 Meade	12	South Portland
Kelly at 2700 block at Water to Water	17	South Portland
3rd dead-end south of Arthur to Meade	40	South Portland
Porter at 2nd into Lair Hill Park	11	South Portland
Woods at southbound Barbur to Woods dead-end at 4th	36	South Portland
Naito southbound down to Grover Street near pedestrian tunnel	23	South Portland
Naito northbound down to Grover Street near pedestrian tunnel	26	South Portland
Grover pedestrian tunnel east end, at Naito/Ross Island Bridge ramp	20	South Portland
Grover pedestrian tunnel west end, at Naito/Ross Island Bridge ramp	19	South Portland
Grover to 1st, west of Naito	16	South Portland
Gibbs dead-end at 2nd to Barbur northbound	50	South Portland

LOCATION	NUMBER OF STEPS	NEIGHBORHOOD
Whitaker dead-end west of Water to Naito northbound	13	South Portland
Whitaker at Barbur southbound to Whitaker at 2nd	28	South Portland
Whitaker west of southbound Barbur to Terwilliger	55	South Portland
Curry dead-end west of Water to Naito northbound	30	South Portland
Curry dead-end west of 1st to Barbur northbound	11	South Portland
1st opposite 3510 (south of Curry) to Barbur northbound	12	South Portland
Abernethy dead-end west of Water to northbound Barbur	9	South Portland
Water dead-end south of Abernethy to northbound Barbur	11	South Portland
Condor west of Barbur: 3 staircases up to sidewalk at 3 homes: 11, 13, and 8 steps respectively	32	South Portland
Condor Lane at Terwilliger to VA Hospital	145	Homestead
Lowell at southbound Barbur to Lowell at View Point Terrace	29	Homestead
Terwilliger at Bancroft to Homestead at Bancroft	35	Homestead
Iowa west of View Point Terrace into greenspace and George Himes Park	129	South Portland
Barbur southbound at Parkhill Drive to Parkhill Drive (Nebraska Steps)	147	Hillsdale
Custer Way and LaView to Custer Way and Kelly	100	South Portland
Service road along I-5 to 4th /5th under Terwilliger viaduct	65	South Burlingame

LOCATION	NUMBER OF STEPS	NEIGHBORHOOD
4th /5th intersection to northbound Terwilliger	41	South Burlingame
4th /5th intersection to Terwilliger ramp to northbound I-5	57	South Burlingame
5th at 7806 to northbound Terwilliger	35	South Burlingame
7836 Terwilliger northeast side of Troy	12	South Burlingame
4th dead-end east of I-5 to Canby and 10th	58	South Burlingame
Balmer Circle at 10056 to Lancaster Road at Ridgeview Lane	50	Marshall Park
Jackson Middle School grounds, cross 40th then via Galeburn right-of-way to 41st	136	West Portland Park
43rd at Primrose to 43rd at Marigold	10	Ashcreek
42nd at Garden Home Road to 42nd north of Hume	48	Multnomah
Multnomah at 3900 block to Garden Home Road west of Capitol Highway	18	Multnomah
Multnomah at 37th to Capitol Highway overpass of Multnomah	24	Multnomah
30th Place north of Canby to Capitol Highway northbound	15	Multnomah
19th south of Evans to southbound Barbur Boulevard at Capitol Hill Road	34	Hillsdale
19th right-of-way between Capitol Hill Road and Evans	10	Hillsdale
Capitol Hill Road to meadow at 19th near Nevada	10	Multnomah
Capitol Hill Road down to Stephens Creek (between Capitol Hill and Bertha)	39	Hillsdale
Bertha Boulevard down to Stephens Creek (between Capitol Hill and Bertha)	26	Hillsdale
Caldew at 805 to Burlingame Avenue	52	Hillsdale

LOCATION	NUMBER OF STEPS	NEIGHBORHOOD
5th opposite 7326 down to westbound Barbur at 5th	36	South Burlingame
Nevada at southbound Barbur to 2nd	16	Hillsdale
23rd north of Kanan to Sunset Drive	20	Hillsdale
Lee dead-end west of 42nd to 43rd over creek	23	Bridlemile
Admiral Court dead-end, over Ivy Creek to 45th north of Beaverton-Hillsdale Highway	17	Bridlemile

Twombly to Melville opposite 4310: a pedestrian path along a right-of-way separated by streets. Railroad tie stairs are interspersed with sections of rough trail, and paved driveway-like portions.
   Melville to Chesapeake: 19
   Chesapeake to Washouga: 28
   Washouga to Twombly: 10
	57	Hillsdale

Chesapeake at 4100 block to Wapato and Fairmount	69	Southwest Hills: Council Crest
Fairmount at 3157 to path leading to dead-end of Council Crest Drive below communications towers	18	Southwest Hills: Council Crest
Hillsboro across from 2750 to Council Crest at Greenway, at water fountain	46	Southwest Hills: Council Crest
Talbot Road to Greenway on Greenway viaduct	25	Southwest Hills: Portland Heights
Montgomery at 2944 to Talbot at 2840, west of Greenway viaduct	51	Southwest Hills: Portland Heights
Montgomery at 2860 to Greenway	86	Southwest Hills: Portland Heights
Greenway opposite 2770 to dead-end of Summit	36	Southwest Hills: Portland Heights
Patton at Vista to Talbot Road	23	Southwest Hills: Portland Heights

LOCATION	NUMBER OF STEPS	NEIGHBORHOOD
Sherwood between 2449 and 2467 to Arden	8	Southwest Hills: Portland Heights
Edgewood Road dead-end to Edgewood Road	23	Southwest Hills: Portland Heights
Broadway Drive at Talbot Place to Ravensview	18	Southwest Hills: Portland Heights
Broadway Drive at 2201 to 2662 Gerald	43	Southwest Hills: Portland Heights
Broadway Drive at 1735 to Terrace Drive at 17th	65	Southwest Hills: Portland Heights
Broadway Drive at 1617 to Davenport	37	Southwest Hills: Portland Heights
Vista at 2530 to Terrace Drive at Elizabeth (accessed at elevated sidewalk that begins at the southeast corner of Vista and Spring)	71	Southwest Hills: Portland Heights
Montgomery Drive at 2575 to Alta Vista Place near Vista	59	Southwest Hills: Portland Heights
Spring to Vista	18	Southwest Hills: Portland Heights
Montgomery Drive at 1698 to Vista	41	Southwest Hills: Portland Heights
North of 1636 Vista down to private steps at Mill Street Terrace	67	Southwest Hills: Portland Heights
Vista at 1456 to Prospect Drive	14	Southwest Hills: Portland Heights
Multi-use path along Sunset Highway to 58th at Canyon Court	28	Sylvan Highlands
Champlain at 2864 to Fairview	81	Arlington Heights
Tichner at 2670 to Parkside Lane	23	Arlington Heights
Washington Park southwest of Marconi Avenue to Parkside Drive	44	Arlington Heights

LOCATION	NUMBER OF STEPS	NEIGHBORHOOD
Apartment building to Cactus Drive dead-end from 1914	14	Goose Hollow: King's Hill
Dead-end of Cactus Drive to Cedar Street (southeast of 2390–2392 Cactus Drive)	36	Goose Hollow: King's Hill
20th along PGE Park, north of Salmon	17	Goose Hollow: King's Hill
20th dead-end south of Jefferson to Market Street Drive, from 1996	82	Goose Hollow
Market Street Drive at 1917 to Mill Street Terrace dead-end	152	Goose Hollow
Market Street Drive at 19th to homes	77	Goose Hollow
13th, between College Street's two levels	69	Goose Hollow
12th at Cardinell to upper level of Cardinell	179	Goose Hollow
10th dead-end at Clifton to Cardinell	57	Goose Hollow
Broadway Drive at 700 block to Hoffman (Elevator Stairs)	203	Southwest Hills

NORTHWEST

Union Station pedestrian bridge	42	Old Town–Chinatown
Glisan at 24th to Westover	51	Northwest District
Irving dead-end west of 24th to Westover	48	Northwest District
25th Place dead-end south of Lovejoy to Westover	41	Northwest District
Lovejoy dead-end west of Marcia Avenue to Summit	33	Northwest District
Marshall dead-end west of 26th to Cornell	55	Northwest District
Northrup dead-end west of 26th to Cornell	63	Northwest District
Summit Avenue south of Summit Court to Westover	157	Hillside
Fairfax west of Cumberland and Westover intersection to Cumberland	131	Hillside

LOCATION	NUMBER OF STEPS	NEIGHBORHOOD
Luray Terrace at 2915 to Luray Circus	52	Hillside
Overton dead-end west of 26th to Cornell	56	Northwest District
Pettygrove west of 27th to Cornell	65	Northwest District
Cornell at 2832 to Summit Avenue	73	Hillside
Quimby at 29th to Cornell	25	Northwest District
Cornell Road at stone tunnel, east end	5	Forest Park
Thurman at 3418 to Aspen	101	Northwest District: Willamette Heights
Macleay Park (Forest Park) to east end, Thurman Street Bridge Steel: 48 Concrete: 23	71	Forest Park
Vaughn dead-end at 30th to Vaughn	32	Northwest District: Willamette Heights
Wardway uphill from Nicolai intersection to Montgomery Park parking lot	57	Northwest Industrial
Wardway at 2856 to 28th Place	36	Northwest District
Bridge Avenue southeast of Saint Johns Bridge to Ridge Trail in Forest Park	48	Linnton
Saint Helens Road (Hwy 30) north of Bridge Avenue stoplight up to Bridge Avenue	70	Linnton
Saint Helens Road (Hwy 30) elevated sidewalk north of Harbor Boulevard to Roseway at 9450	80	Linnton
Saint Helens Road (Hwy 30) at 9663 (not marked) to Roseway	67	Linnton
Saint Helens Road (Hwy 30) at Hoge to path leading to Roseway dead-end at 10131	44	Linnton
Saint Helens Road (Hwy 30) to elevated sidewalk downhill of intersection of Wilark and Hoge avenues	10	Linnton

LOCATION	NUMBER OF STEPS	NEIGHBORHOOD
Saint Helens Road (Hwy 30) to Wilark dead-end	41	Linnton
Saint Helens Road (Hwy 30) north of 105th Avenue to 2nd Street dead-end	106	Linnton
107th Avenue at Saint Helens Road (Hwy 30) to 3rd Street	176	Linnton
2nd Street at 108th Avenue to 3rd Street	92	Linnton
2nd Street at 109th Avenue to 3rd Street	57	Linnton
Meridian Ridge Drive to Skyline Boulevard (300 block)	167	Forest Park

NORTHEAST

Mason and 19th to Crane	51	Sabin
Ridgewood Drive at 24th to Stuart Drive at Alameda	75	Alameda
Stuart Drive at 25th to 2644 Alameda	70	Alameda
Fremont at 3011 to Alameda Terrace	98	Alameda
Fremont west of 32nd to Alameda Terrace	65	Alameda
38th at 3041 (at Wistaria) to Alameda	78	Beaumont-Wilshire
Wistaria at 4131 to Alameda	127	Beaumont-Wilshire
Wistaria at 4243 to Alameda	118	Beaumont-Wilshire
Wistaria at 49th to Wistaria Drive east of 48th	30	Rose City Park
50th dead-end north of Sandy Boulevard to Wistaria	43	Rose City Park
51st dead-end north of Sandy Boulevard to Wistaria	50	Rose City Park
Columbia Boulevard ramp to 33rd southbound	23	Concordia
42nd south of Halsey to pedestrian bridge over I-84	25	Hollywood

LOCATION	NUMBER OF STEPS	NEIGHBORHOOD
42nd at Senate to pedestrian bridge over I-84	28	Laurelhurst

SOUTHEAST

LOCATION	NUMBER OF STEPS	NEIGHBORHOOD
Colonel Summers Park to dead-end of 18th south of Belmont	23	Buckman
Bush at 8th to northbound McLoughlin	16	Brooklyn
24th dead-end to Holgate eastbound	11	Brooklyn
24th dead-end to Holgate westbound	9	Brooklyn
26th Place to eastbound Tacoma, east end of Tacoma overpass of McLoughlin	50	Ardenwald–Johnson Creek
McLoughlin southbound to westbound Tacoma, west end of Tacoma overpass over McLoughlin	39	Sellwood-Moreland
McLoughlin northbound to Tacoma westbound, east end of Tacoma overpass of McLoughlin	50	Ardenwald–Johnson Creek
McLoughlin southbound to Tacoma eastbound, west end of Tacoma overpass of McLoughlin	34	Sellwood-Moreland
Ash at 65th to Thorburn	61	Mount Tabor
Belmont at 66th Place to Yamhill Court	31	Mount Tabor
Belmont at 67th to Yamhill at 67th	21	Mount Tabor
Belmont at 67th to Scott Drive and Morrison	18	Mount Tabor
Taylor and 71st to Mount. Tabor Park	25	Mount Tabor

NORTH

LOCATION	NUMBER OF STEPS	NEIGHBORHOOD
Going to Greeley, west side	77	Overlook
Going to Greeley, east side	31	Overlook
Peninsular at Houghton	14	Kenton

WILLAMETTE RIVER BRIDGE STAIRS

LOCATION	NUMBER OF STEPS
Broadway, west side; Naito Parkway to eastbound sidewalk	81
Broadway, west side; Naito Parkway to westbound sidewalk	82
Broadway, west side; ramp down to lower level of Broadway north of Johnson	26
Broadway, west side; ramp at Irving	18
Broadway, east side; Interstate southbound to eastbound sidewalk	27
Steel, west side; Naito to top deck	47
Steel, east side; Eastbank Esplanade south of the bridge via a pedestrian overpass of rail tracks to Lloyd Boulevard southbound, past Oregon intersection	65
Burnside, west side; 1st to eastbound sidewalk	30
Burnside, west side; 1st to westbound sidewalk	31
Burnside, east side; Esplanade to eastbound sidewalk	86
Morrison, west side; north of Morrison between Naito and 1st	23
Morrison, west side; 1st to Alder, east of 2nd	14
Morrison, west side; 1st to Washington	14
Morrison, west side; between Naito and 1st south of Stark to ramp	25
Morrison, east side; Water and Morrison intersection to westbound bridge approach lanes (east of I-5)	49
Morrison, east side; westbound bridge approach, hanging stairs: descending (30) under the approach and ascending (25) the other side (west of I-5, above the Esplanade)	55

LOCATION	NUMBER OF STEPS
Morrison, east side; westbound lane, hanging stairs: descending (29) to pass under a northbound I-5 ramp (25) and ascending to continue west onto the bridge sidewalk (east of Water)	54
Morrison, east side; Water and Belmont intersection up to eastbound bridge ramp	42
Hawthorne, west side; Waterfront Park up to westbound sidewalk	36
Hawthorne, west side; Waterfront Park up to eastbound sidewalk	37
Hawthorne, west side; southbound Naito to westbound bridge ramp	23
Hawthorne, west side; southbound Naito to eastbound bridge	23
Hawthorne, east side; Esplanade to ramp leading to westbound sidewalk	7
Hawthorne, east side; Madison and Water intersection up to westbound bridge approach (east of I-5)	45
Hawthorne, east side; Hawthorne Boulevard at 1st up to eastbound bridge ramp	50
Hawthorne, east side; Hawthorne Boulevard at 3rd to southbound ramp heading toward Martin Luther King Jr Boulevard	45
Hawthorne, east side; ramp from Esplanade leading to eastbound sidewalk	7
Sellwood, west side; multi-use river path to westbound sidewalk	11
Sellwood, east side; rail road tracks to westbound sidewalk	45

PORTLAND PARK STAIRS

LOCATION	NUMBER OF STEPS	PARK
SOUTHWEST		
Brick steps along west edge of park	25	Pioneer Courthouse Square
Salmon Street Springs	14	Governor Tom McCall Waterfront Park
Fountain	31	Keller Fountain Park
Fountain	25	Lovejoy Fountain Park
Burnside at 24th Place to *Coming of the White Man* statue above Washington Way, marked "Stearns Road Trail to Rose Garden"	280	Washington Park
Osage dead-end south of Burnside to Lewis and Clark Drive	175	Washington Park
NORTHWEST		
Stairs down to metal walkway over water	11	Tanner Springs Park
Fountain steps; water emerges at top of risers	4	Jamison Square
NORTHEAST		
Stone staircase, north end of summit	72	Rocky Butte
Railroad tie–rebar steps alongside stone wall used by climbers, below summit, west side	33	Rocky Butte
SOUTHEAST		
Ankeny opposite 3437: brick staircase down into park	88	Laurelhurst Park
Park road to Reservoir 1	81	Mount Tabor Park
60th south of Hawthorne to Reservoir 6	43	Mount Tabor Park
Reservoir 6 to Reservoir 5	134	Mount Tabor Park

LOCATION	NUMBER OF STEPS	PARK
69th dead-end south of Yamhill to Mount Tabor summit	282	Mount Tabor Park
Steps down from 43rd and Powell into park's northwest corner	35	Creston Park
Swimming pool to terrace above	60	Creston Park
Steps down from entrance to spring fed pond	23	Crystal Springs Rhododendron Garden

NORTH

Sunken Rose Garden; brick stairs at four compass points leading down into garden
  North stairs: 18
  East stairs: 13
  South stairs: 18
  West stairs: 13
	62	Peninsula Park

Under Saint Johns Bridge up to Edison	41	Cathedral Park

NOT A STAIR BUT . . .

If you like stairs, you might enjoy these other places that exist beyond the dead-end sign. The city maintains 22 pedestrian bridges over creeks, canyons, or roads. Two of my favorites are near schools:

 SW Spring Street's dead-end west of Vista leads to a pedestrian bridge over a canyon. On the other side is Saint Helens Court, a beautiful street. This bridge, built in 1938, serves kids who attend nearby Ainsworth Elementary.

 SW 25th Avenue south of Martha is a pedestrian bridge bringing kids to Robert Gray Middle School in the Hillsdale neighborhood. The 25th Avenue span, while traversing exquisite terrain, resembles a prison yard, with caging installed after one adventurous teenager successfully rappelled from it in the 1980s. It was built in 1978.

When Interstate 5 was constructed in the 1950s through Portland, it excised some residential streets. Pedestrian bridges, narrow butterfly-bandages of a solution, were constructed over the freeway to help heal the incision through once-contiguous neighborhoods. They aren't scenic, but interesting in terms of access. Here are two:

 N Bryant Street over Interstate 5. In early 2010, plans were to renovate this pedestrian bridge to eliminate its cagelike aspect.

The N Bryant Street pedestrian/bike overpass of Interstate 5.

A staircase cat watches warily for more intruders, assessing each before allowing contact.

■▬ N Failing Street over Interstate 5. This pedestrian bridge
was closed for a time in the 1990s as neighbors on one side
claimed that criminals used it for quick escapes onto the
other side of the bridge.

Another intriguing, hidden pedestrian bridge is on N Con-
cord Avenue, over Going Street. Going is the main conduit onto
Swan Island, and it's a virtual freeway here. This bridge appears
magically at the end of quiet neighborhood streets in the bluffs
above the bustle.

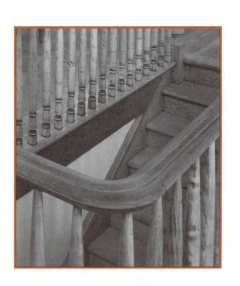

Index

ABOUT THE AUTHOR

LAURA O. FOSTER writes about exploring Portland, Oregon, and the small towns around it. With its river beaches, volcanic peaks, forested mountain chain, and hundreds of stairways in old interconnected neighborhoods, Portland is a pedestrian nirvana. In her books Laura investigates off-the-beaten-path places—their geology, architecture, trees, and human inhabitants, and weaves these diverse threads together to tell the many stories in one of the nation's most livable cities. For each walking exploration, she slows it down to stop in a neighborhood's center, to eat, drink, shop, read, or otherwise soak in the local scene.

Laura is also the author of *Portland Hill Walks* (2005) and *Portland City Walks* (2008). When she's not writing about Portland, she's creating new urban adventures or leading walks for local governments, civic groups, and nonprofits. She lives in rural Northwest Portland where her dog and youngest daughter have taught her the joys of running barefoot in the woods.